What people are saying about ...

SACRED SURRENDER

"Jaime has been gifted by God with a heart for ministry. Her voice is as beautiful as her teaching! She is a game changer in bringing people closer to Jesus."

Karen Kingsbury, #1 *New York Times* bestselling author

"Waiting is one of my least favorite activities. In *Sacred Surrender*, Jaime Jamgochian reminds us that waiting is never wasted when we release our in-between seasons to the Lord. If you want to see your hard transformed into holy, pick up this book today!"

Melissa Spoelstra, Bible study author and teacher, author of *Angels*, *The Gospel of John*, and *Isaiah*

"To *wait* means 'to hope, anticipate, and trust.' *Sacred Surrender* richly embodies this idea and shows us how waiting well can deepen our faith and our character. Through her sacrifices, victories, and setbacks, my friend Jaime Jamgochian has learned the importance of placing her hope and trust passionately in Jesus, anticipating His love when the frustration of waiting sets in. She shows us there's something beautiful to gain in every season of waiting."

Lynette Lewis, author, TEDx speaker, CEO of MyWhyLife

"Jaime Jamgochian's love for Jesus is palpable—plus, she oozes authenticity. She combines gospel-centered worship and narrative with such genuine warmth it both engages and inspires whoever has the blessing of being within the sound of her voice!"

Lisa Harper, bestselling author and speaker

"It can be difficult to always be full of faith while waiting—waiting for healing, waiting for an answer from God, or just waiting for something to change in your life. Jaime Jamgochian has given us a gift in this book that helps us learn how to surrender to the love of God and find new ways to live in joy and deepen our faith during our seasons of waiting. I have personally witnessed how she has exercised faith and a joyful attitude during her seasons of waiting, and I know she will encourage you to wait well and see God move in your life during the process."

Alex Seeley, cofounder of The Belonging Co Church, author of *Tailor Made* and *The Opposite Life*

"Few voices can sing the truths of faith and suffering like Jaime Jamgochian—and now, she writes them with equal beauty and boldness. *Sacred Surrender* is an anthem of perseverance for every woman who finds herself in the in-between: waiting on God, grieving what was lost, or holding on to promises yet unseen. Jaime's words are tender but strong, personal yet deeply scriptural. If your story holds sorrow or surrender, this book will help you worship through the waiting and discover the holy invitation hidden in hardship."

Heather M. Dixon, national speaker and founder of The Rescued Letters Collective, author of *Determined: Living Like Jesus in Every Moment*

SACRED SURRENDER

SACRED SURRENDER

The Practice of Waiting Well with God

JAIME JAMGOCHIAN

150 YEARS STRONG
DAVID C COOK

SACRED SURRENDER
Published by Esther Press,
an imprint of David C Cook
4050 Lee Vance Drive
Colorado Springs, CO 80918 U.S.A.

Integrity Music Limited, a Division of David C Cook
Brighton, East Sussex BN1 2RE, England

Bible credits are listed at the back of the book.

Library of Congress Control Number 2025940626
ISBN 978-0-8307-8823-1
eISBN 978-0-8307-8824-8

Published in association with the Books & Such Literary
Management, www.booksandsuch.com.

The Team: Susan McPherson, Julie Cantrell, James Hershberger,
Brian Mellema, Jack Campbell, Brittany Stonestreet, Susan Murdock
Cover Design: Micah Kandros
Cover Author Bio Photo: Alaina Broyles Photography

Printed in the United States of America
First Edition 2025

1 2 3 4 5 6 7 8 9 10

070725

To all those who find themselves
in a season of waiting.

CONTENTS

Foreword by Susie Larson 11

Introduction 15

Chapter 1: When Hard Becomes Holy 21

Chapter 2: Words Carry Weight 43

Chapter 3: When Hope Has Been Hijacked 63

Chapter 4: God's Timetable Is on Time 81

Chapter 5: When Your Plan B Is God's Plan A 99

Chapter 6: The Thoughts We Think 115

Chapter 7: Grateful through the Wait 135

Chapter 8: When God Wants You to Grow 153

Chapter 9: More Love, Less Fear 173

Chapter 10: Will You Wait Well? 193

Conclusion: A Final Note from Jaime 213

Acknowledgments 217

Notes 219

Bible Credits 221

FOREWORD

I met my friend Jaime over fifteen years ago when I spoke at an event where she was leading worship. We became fast friends. Jaime's joy and passion for Jesus were the most noticeable aspects of her. I battled Lyme disease and then later, severe mold toxicity, which made traveling to events challenging for me. She showed such care and compassion for me. Little did we both know that Jaime would face the same diagnosis in the following years.

Our shared love for Jesus and fierce health battles have profoundly intertwined our hearts. We've spent considerable time waiting on God, contending for breakthroughs, and discovering His faithfulness. Waiting on God is hard sometimes, and navigating a life that differs from your expectations isn't easy. You've got to keep hope alive while embracing grace for the difficult present moments. You've got to avoid negativity like the plague while admitting that empty positivity can also be toxic.

Being honest about your struggle while daring to surrender to a God who is faithful is not for the faint of heart. The temptation to strive in your own strength is strong. The call to trust God and His strength is supernatural, but at times, it feels unnatural. Yet, it's the only way forward.

I once heard about a little sheep that repeatedly wandered away from the flock. She loved her Shepherd, but her curiosity and yearning compelled her to leave His side. One day, she strayed too far and found herself stuck in the thicket. The more she pulled to free herself, the more she injured her leg. The thorns punctured her skin, and the pressure broke her little leg. She was stuck, lonely, hurt, and afraid. She closed her eyes and whimpered when, suddenly, she saw the Shepherd in the distance! He'd come for her!

The Good Shepherd freed her from her snare and carried her home on His shoulders. In fact, He carried her every single day until she fully recovered. Something miraculous occurred during that time. Her little heart began beating in rhythm with His. She developed an attachment to her Shepherd and couldn't bear the thought of leaving His side. Her pain and His care cultivated a deep, abiding intimacy.

When life doesn't turn out the way you hoped, it's tempting to take matters into your own hands. The temptation to preempt outcomes, take control, and self-sabotage can be overwhelming even before you realize what you've done. While waiting for a change or a breakthrough, some wander from their Shepherd through decadent, indulgent living. They numb their pain, postpone their breakthrough, and reinforce their captivity. Most people don't wait well.

Still, others may strive in their own strength while waiting for their breakthrough. They forsake the holy process of waiting and force outcomes far inferior to what God would have given them had they waited on Him and trusted His goodness.

I think it's fair to say that both Jaime and I are passionate and driven enough that if it weren't for God's presence and goodness amid our struggles, we might have been the ones who strived to make life happen. We may have run hard and run ourselves right into the ground. But our weakness made us dependent. Our struggle made us strong. It's not that God made us sick or orchestrated our suffering, but He certainly redeemed it and used it to transform us into vessels He can fill and spill.

Jaime's new book, *Sacred Surrender*, is filled with hard-won wisdom. She doesn't offer platitudes that mean nothing to her. Instead, she provides insight from the valley, wisdom from her suffering, and perspective from her pain. She understands a lot about waiting on God. She's learned the secret of surrender and the power of worship in those in-between seasons.

Walk with Jaime through these pages, and you'll find her to be a compassionate, accessible friend. Take her wisdom to heart, and see if you don't discover God, intimately, on your own journey. Read about how God fulfilled some of the desires of her heart, and dare to start dreaming once more about your own possibilities.

Waiting well requires spiritual maturity. Trusting God, even when our flesh wants to take over, demands a certain grit. What if you dared to trust God on a deeper level during this season of your life? What if you opened your clenched fists and offered God the thing you're holding on to so tightly? Humble surrender leads to intimacy with God and an eventual breakthrough in your circumstances. God treasures your faith and cherishes your trust. He's worthy of it, and He's worth the wait. He knows what He's doing with your life. Let Him meet you in those tender places. Dare to believe He's kinder and more loving than you ever imagined Him to be. I'll be praying for you as you move into this next season with a newfound heart to trust and surrender all to the God who loves you.

Enjoy the journey.

Susie Larson
Bestselling author
Talk radio host
National speaker

INTRODUCTION

Whether our paths have crossed at a concert or a women's event in the last twenty years, or you have been listening to my music for decades or days, or we're meeting for the first time ... THANK YOU for picking up this book. I've never believed that anything is coincidental, but rather, everything happens by divine appointment. So, I believe that is how you stumbled upon this book. I am thrilled to know you will be diving into the pages ahead. If I am being really honest, I never thought I would be writing a book, but after years of watching God's plans unfold completely different from how I envisioned they would, I am excited to put words and thoughts on paper and in a format other than song lyrics.

My greatest prayer is that these chapters, filled with my personal journey of faith, real-life stories, and hopefully some wisdom I have gained along the way, will help you recognize that you are not alone as you navigate the great wait and the in-between seasons of life. I pray your heart is encouraged and challenged, and that you find yourself growing in deeper intimacy with the Lord as you turn every page. I hope that you find much of your own story along the way and that we can walk out this crazy, amazing faith journey together.

The greatest faith action I have learned through the low valley seasons as well as the mountaintop seasons is to worship in the waiting and truly grasp the art of surrender. I remember hearing the word "surrender" as a new follower of Christ in my early twenties and thinking, *Well, that's easy! You just give everything to God, right?* I quickly realized that a truly surrendered life unto Him is not all butterflies and roses. Actually, there are times when it will feel more like dragons and thorns as we fight the enemy along the path we are called to take. It will require sacrificing our own flesh and our old ways of thinking. Choosing not to place trust in our own plans is a heart posture of obedience. It takes time, practice, patience, and work, just as anything in life does, to learn how to wholeheartedly surrender. Sometimes it will take all you have to just keep standing when everything inside of you wants to disappear to a sunny ocean island where all your cares of this world can fade away, even if for a brief moment.

After long seasons of believing and waiting for precious promises from God to come to pass (that have yet to), I realized that it was time to start living to the fullest in the in-between and empty places. It has become my life mantra that it is still possible to find joy and live fully even in the most barren places. I finally booked the dream trip solo, recognizing that Jesus is the best date since He knows the deepest desires of my heart. I finally started seeing myself through His lens instead of how the world perceives me. Although I have had the honor of achieving career goals and dreams, that has not come without a cost. But that is all part of this walk of faith. Trials will threaten to knock us down from time to time, but we can choose whether they crush us or refine us.

When I first began to walk out this journey of faith in Christ, many of my lifelong dreams started to happen very quickly. I was a jazz pianist studying at Berklee College of Music when I met the Lord, and soon after, my heart and song completely changed. All I wanted to do was sing for Him. I literally lived out the message of this book very early on in my walk. Even though I always envisioned myself recording, touring, and signing to a label, I laid those dreams down when I came to faith in Jesus. I wanted to know Christ more and be a true disciple of His. That became my soul focus and one goal. When I graduated college, instead of heading to LA or NYC like most of my music-loving peers, God placed it on my heart to move to Seattle to attend a two-year Bible leadership school. It appeared backward career wise, but I continued to feel that tug of the Spirit, and in obeying His lead, I learned my first act of complete surrender. *"Not my will, Lord, but Yours be done"* was my true heart's cry.

All I wanted to do was sing for Him.

I mean, Seattle, Washington, was not really a hub of music in my eyes, but God had a greater plan. He always examines the heart and is most concerned about who we are becoming over any career status or earthly achievements. I came alive in Seattle, learning all about the Bible and ministry. I started to lead worship for the first time and genuinely fell in love with it. I also realized the songs I wanted to sing were songs for Him. I can honestly say I had laid down all of my former dreams on the altar and was completely content serving the Lord at this incredible church He had brought me to. My heart was fully surrendered, and I believe that is where God always begins His best work. Before I even had time to process it all, I was signing my first Christian record deal, releasing music, and going out to tour in His way, His time, and His plan. Surrender is a sacred and holy invitation from the Lord and for our highest good. It is an act of true worship to lay down the things that we hold most dear, willingly put our hearts in the Lord's hands, and say, "It's all Yours, Jesus. Take my life and let it be a sacrifice of praise unto You."

Surrender is a sacred and holy invitation from the Lord and for our highest good.

Maybe you're reading this while feeling stuck in a specific area of your life, or maybe your heart is discouraged as you are in what seems to be a never-ending cycle of praying for breakthrough. Or perhaps you feel like you have surrendered the same thing to Jesus over and over, but truthfully, you're still holding on to it. We will chat about that in the chapters ahead. I hope to offer you practical tools and guided prayers as you navigate those waters. You see, just like many of you, I may have some life experience in this area, but I am still quick to forget. I must remind myself and pull my heart back in a posture of surrender often.

We will dive deep into seasons of waiting and the in-between. Why, you may ask? Because waiting is a universal struggle. We are *all* waiting on something. When you search *#waiting* on Instagram, you will see that it has more than nine million hits. Our life can seem hijacked, and prayers can seem to go unanswered. Everyone experiences the in-between waiting seasons at some point. I hope these pages will show you how to wait well by changing the lens from only seeing the difficult parts to trusting in God's holy work.

There is a phrase I clung to during one of the most challenging seasons of my life, and still do: "If it's not good yet, then maybe God's not done yet." I have learned that the very nature of our God is that He is good, so as we begin to change the filter through which we see things, then our everyday lives become a lot more beautiful, especially in the waiting.

"If it's not good yet, then maybe God's not done yet."

Before you start reading this book, would you do me a favor and open your hands to God like you are receiving a gift? Close your eyes and take a moment to take a deep breath. Our lives can become so full and cluttered at times that we forget to practice thoughtful breathing. Now, release anything to Him that immediately comes to mind that is weighing you down or distracting you. If I were sitting next to you right now, I would sing the chorus of my song "Release." I put the words below and hope that they will bring your heart peace as you continue to surrender it all to Him.

Release rest and let it go trusting in His perfect plan
And breathe 'cause He is in control
Surrender is the path to peace
Release.[1]

As you begin to dive into the pages ahead, pray this prayer with me: *"God, would You speak to my heart through this book and show me how to live a sacred surrendered life unto You."*

Surrendered together,
Jaime Jamgochian

Chapter 1

WHEN HARD BECOMES HOLY

When I heard the words "Lyme disease" come out of the doctor's mouth, I sat in complete shock. How was that even possible? Doesn't that come from a tick bite?

I didn't recall getting bit. I strongly dislike camping (mainly because of bugs!), and I would rather book a hotel on the beach any day of the week. And no … I am not a diva! The doctor explained, and tests confirmed, that however it happened, my body was starting to shut down, and my life would take a drastic turn because of this disease. The news rocked me to my core. I was confused, scared, and honestly wondered what this meant for the future I had planned out in my mind. This was certainly not part of it. A chronic disease that affected many organs and parts of my body? How could this be happening?

Have you ever found yourself in a shocking moment like mine? Whatever your diagnosis, dream deferred, or dreadful news, no one is ever fully prepared. We never see it coming, right? I mean, I had maintained a healthy lifestyle prior to this diagnosis, so this was impossible to predict. I know people who eat fast food every week who appear to be healthier than me.

Have you ever found yourself in a similar situation? Maybe it was a relationship that went sour or someone who deeply wounded you. Maybe it was a dream you worked so hard to build that ended up crumbling. Are you the woman who shows up at every baby shower to celebrate your friends but still longs for a child of your own? Or are you the girl who has been a bridesmaid twenty-seven times but not yet the bride? I feel the pain you are experiencing. The pain of the "in-between, hanging out in limbo, feels like it will never end" season. But I have an important question to ask you: Are you *STILL standing*? If so, I bet you have a little more strength and a little more grit than you did before the trial that intended to break you actually forged a fire inside that wouldn't have been there otherwise.

This journey of faith is not easy. Then again, we were never promised easy. However, this faith journey, with every high and every low, is absolutely worth it. You see, it was not long ago that I came out of a season in which everything that could be stripped from me was taken away. YET, I am still standing and learning every day how to truly surrender. I believe you, too, will be standing with a new posture and surrendering like never before until your own in-between season or difficult circumstance has passed. And it will pass.

Facing the Unknown

Once I was thrust into this new reality, I began doing any and all research I possibly could. I was determined to fight this and come out stronger on the other side. Here are several facts about the disease that I learned quickly. First, you don't have to remember being bitten since tick bites are small and can look like a little blackhead or freckle. Second, when you have Lyme disease you may look the same on the outside, but you will feel like you have mono mixed with the flu, along with some of the worst headaches you've ever experienced. Also, while your body is under some kind of physical attack, you might also experience neurological issues, joint pain, muscle weakness, anxiety, and depression. While symptoms can show up differently for each person, it is a very tricky and nasty disease.

While sickness is often a part of our lives, I don't believe that God is the one who inflicts disease on people. He is a good Father, and a good dad would never willingly put sickness on his child. I believe sickness is on earth because of the state of the fallen world we live in. What I do know to be true, however, is that God will use everything (and I mean *everything*) for our good. It was when I was living in this in-between place where I sensed God inviting me in to one of the hardest seasons of my life and, paradoxically, one of the most holy. This was the beginning of my journey of what it really meant to live a life that was surrendered to God. I thought I had been living this way, but when everything that feels "normal" or comfortable begins to be taken away one by one, you get to see how surrendered your heart actually is. When you do not like your circumstances you have several choices: ignore them, try to run from them, or gently begin to embrace the beauty of where you are, even if it does not look beautiful at the time. This is a holy invitation to lay down all your preconceived notions about where you think your life should be and what it should look like. *Holiness* is not a word that is used much in the church anymore, but it is a setting apart from sin and being dedicated unto God. God has a way of turning our most desperate situations into the deepest places of intimacy with Him if we will allow Him to.

Now that I'm on the other side, I can confidently and humbly say that I learned how to thrive and fully live my life even while in the hidden seasons. I also learned the power of true rest, how to effectively pray, and that God is still so, so good even when our circumstances are not.

The Reality That Changed Everything

In the beginning of this journey, I tried to ignore all the symptoms and push them down ... push them away. I optimistically thought I could keep my regular tour schedule, work part time at my church, and do all the normal things I'd done before this diagnosis, until I woke up one day and could no longer function. I hit a wall. I literally reached my body's limit, and it no longer worked the way it did before. I remember lying in my bed asking, "God, why me?"

I had been traveling, singing, speaking, and pastoring people at my church and seeing them come to Jesus—why would this be happening to *me*? Somewhere deep in my heart I believed the lie that if you serve God and surrender your life to Him, then you would be excluded from the hard trials in life. Can I be honest with you? I don't believe the church talks enough about the pain and agony Jesus endured, and how we will face our own trials and suffering if we call ourselves true followers of Christ. Believers are *not* exempt from suffering. In fact, if we are living a surrendered life to the Lord, we are more of a target to the enemy, which is why we have to stay alert and on guard. But more on that in another chapter ...

Somewhere deep in my heart I believed the lie that if you serve God and surrender your life to Him, then you would be excluded from the hard trials in life.

I went from doctor to doctor and from treatment to treatment. I followed numerous health protocols regarding diet, supplements, medicine, and more. Spiritually speaking, many people prayed for me and laid hands on me. I focused on inner spiritual healing, regularly asking God if I had unforgiveness in my heart or if there was anything that might be causing my body to be sick. I begged God to heal me, but despite all I was doing, things continued to get worse.

During that time, I wish someone would've had the courage to look me in the eye and tell me this truth: "I can promise that if you embrace the hard and not-so-perfect seasons of your life, you will find Jesus in a new way and with a greater depth because of what you are walking through. You will enter into a place with Him that few others ever get to experience. This season is excruciating, but it's also an honor to walk through it with a God who will never leave your side. It *can* be holy." You see, He and I grew closer than I ever thought possible while in the trenches of the most challenging season I've ever faced. He was still with me and He was still for me in the midst of all I was going through, and that reality changed everything.

When you find yourself suffering in some way, I truly believe you walk on holy ground in the unknown, in-between places of life. Jesus becomes your every breath, your only strength, and the One who whispers, "Will you trust Me? I am still with you and for you, and even in this hard place, there is beauty to be found." Whether healing comes on earth or in heaven, He promises to heal us, and that promise is enough to rest upon. Sometimes I wonder if we want the Healer as much as we desire the healing or the Giver as much as the gifts He gives. I think it is important to ask ourselves during desperate seasons if Christ is enough. Our Christian culture here in the Western world can, at times, be more about what we can get from God instead of who He is and what He has done in our lives through His Son. We must learn that when we are sifted or pruned by the hand of God that it is not a bad thing but, instead, a way that He is drawing us even closer to Himself and causing our faith to grow in new ways.

Jesus becomes your every breath, your only strength, and the One who whispers, "Will you trust Me? I am still with you and for you, and even in this hard place, there is beauty to be found."

During that season of my life, I stopped everything familiar and comfortable, including my church staff position and traveling and touring. I put a new music project on hold. I sold the condo that I owned and had recently redecorated and moved north to live with my parents in order to receive additional medical treatment and to rest and heal. Talk about a humbling season. I went from being busy to having no plans, and from singing to crying. I went from health to seeking healing, and from joy to wondering if I'd ever laugh again.

Prior to all this, I didn't know anything about the toll that chronic pain takes on your body and your mind. I salute anyone reading this who wakes up every day and chooses to live, while being in some kind of physical pain. You are my hero. The Bible says that "we have the mind of Christ" (1 Cor. 2:16) and that we are to "put on the full armor of God" (Eph. 6:13). During that season of being home and going through many treatments, I discovered something. I realized that if the enemy was able to shut my voice down through physical illness, then he would also try to shut my spirit down through discouragement, depression, and despair. For a while, it almost worked. I had to remind myself daily that God still had a specific purpose for my life.

I realized that if the enemy was able to shut my voice down through physical illness, then he would also try to shut my spirit down through discouragement, depression, and despair.

The Purpose in Pain

When you go through tribulation or an in-between season, you will inevitably feel opposition. However, that opposition is not there to stop you from moving forward but to help you overcome. When we press on regardless of what we're facing, we gain ground and authority in more areas of our lives. As believers, we don't get to treat God as though He's a genie, expecting Him to answer our every prayer exactly how we prayed it. Our faith doesn't work that way. Instead, our prayer should be to do the will of our Father. My friend, we do not see things here on earth the way God sees them. Our part is to live a surrendered, holy life unto our King, and to trust Him.

So, I ask you this: What do *you* need to surrender to the Lord? Is there something or someone that needs to be brought to the foot of the cross? I know it can be painful to let go of the things we think we want or need. Sometimes it is self-pity, victimhood, rejection, or fear that we need to release. These are all distractions that can pull us away from the real meaning of our purpose here on earth: to grow more like Jesus and to extend the love we've received from Him to the people we encounter.

Something beautiful happens when He invites us into deep waters in which all we can say is, "God, I trust You." That can be a gut-wrenching statement when nothing makes sense but the truth of His love for you. Maybe you need to start declaring that out loud every day. Allowing the truth of God's Word to be heard by your ears and to sink deep down into your heart.

Something beautiful happens when He invites us into deep waters in which all we can say is, "God, I trust You."

I have learned that every trial has an expiration date. Things might not end how or when you want them to, but we live in times and seasons. Nothing lasts forever except eternity, but God promises to be with us every step of the way in this life. As believers, we often pray prayers that sound like "Jesus, make me more like You," and we sing songs with verses that say "I trust You no matter what." So why are we surprised when the trials of life come in order for us to become more like Him? Challenges that will refine us, convict us, and change us. *Holiness* is a word you rarely hear in the modern-day church, but isn't that the goal of running our race?

On the Road to Holy

It is the hard that makes us holy. Easy does not typically produce growth. It is difficulty that challenges us to press in to Jesus. When I had to take a sabbatical from working and receive ongoing treatments at a Lyme center in Huntington, New York, I honestly felt like my life was taking many steps backward. In the natural (world), it certainly appeared that way. Leave my familiar home to move back in with my folks? Leave a job I love? Stop doing what I am most passionate about: traveling, singing, and ministering as my career? In some ways, I felt like a teenager living at home again with my parents and relying on them to take care of me. It was HARD, and it was HUMBLING. If you are in that season right now, my biggest piece of advice would be to fully embrace it. Allow God to do the work in and through you in that broken, but beautiful, place.

James 4:6 says, "God opposes the proud but gives grace to the humble" (ESV). During a season of hard, you will most likely feel humbled in many different ways. Maybe your body won't be able to do what it always naturally did. This can be very humbling. Maybe you won't have the energy to keep up with the schedule you once had. That can be very humbling. Or maybe you feel like everyone is looking at you and wondering why you are walking through something so difficult. I sure felt that from time to time. You wonder what people are saying or thinking about you. That can be incredibly humbling. One of the things I have learned, though, is that a humble and contrite heart is what God seems to want the most. Maybe it is because He knows if we are not relying on our own strength and abilities, then we will be resting and relying on Him. It requires strength and focused commitment to say (and really mean), "Not my will but Your will be done, Father," when you are walking through a season that makes no sense in the natural. I have noticed something, though. Most people I know who are making big splashes in the kingdom of God and seeing good fruit in their lives all have this one thing in common: God entrusted them to walk through a hard season that caused them to be humbled in many ways. There is a pruning that happens when we are walking through a difficult situation, which causes the dead and dying things in our lives to fall to the ground and be stripped away. If you are being humbled in a particular area, do not resist it but rather lean even further into the ways that God is shaping you through that challenging time. Our roots are forced to grow deeper when things are being shaken up on the surface. Most of the time, God is cutting off the branches in our lives that are not bearing the best fruit. Yield instead of resisting and rest instead of striving if you find yourself in this place.

For some, it might require you to stop ignoring the hard, the hurt, and the pain and really bring it to the feet of Jesus for the first time. I want to encourage you to pour out your heart to Him like King David shows us in the book of Psalms. He was so vulnerable and raw before the Lord. He held nothing back.

One of the most powerful things my pastor once said to me was, "It's okay to tell God how you really feel about something." The truth is, He already knows everything that is going on in our hearts because He created them. He knows our thoughts before we even think them, and He knows our words before we speak them. So, pour it *all* out to Him. Then, ask Him this question: "What in this hard situation are You trying to do to make me more holy?" Sit with that thought and see how He responds.

Maybe it will be a gentle nudge or a thought that there is some type of action you need to take. Maybe you need to apologize to someone or forgive yourself. Maybe He will lead you to a scripture to stand on during your difficult season. Whatever you do, don't stop there. Don't give in to the temptation to set up camp in the defeat, disappointment, guilt, shame, or whatever you are facing. Allow the Holy Spirit to help you to move through it and to keep running when you feel like retreating.

You might be wondering how that's possible when the circumstances don't seem to be changing. Well, that, my friend, is where the real work comes in. Your heart posture will shift, your perspective will begin to change, and your surrender will cause the situation to seem lighter even while you're still in the trenches.

Embracing What I Never Wanted

I can share from my own personal experience that what I walked through paved the way for things that no longer mattered to be stripped away. My heart changed. I began to see Jesus in a new way ... as a friend who understood suffering and pain because He carried it all to the cross for me.

- I learned that loneliness could be turned into alone time with God.
- I learned that His presence really was more than enough.
- I learned that He is rerouting my circumstances to line up my life with His purpose.

The word I sensed in my spirit for that season that got me through was *I am rerouting you.* It still did not make sense to me at that moment, but now that several years have passed since that trial, I can look back and say, "WOW, God, You really DID reroute my entire direction."

The word I sensed in my spirit for that season that got me through was ***I am rerouting you.***

God saw a brand-new season where I would be back in Christian music. Touring, releasing albums, and hearing my songs back on the radio. He had placed those gifts and dreams in my heart, so why couldn't He resurrect them? Let me be clear that they had *all* been stripped away and looked completely dead and over. But this is the foundation of our faith in Christ, right? He is the resurrected King who was dead and came back to life. He can redeem and restore anything He chooses. There is absolutely nothing that He cannot make new.

God's dreams for our lives are bigger than our own dreams. I began to pray this prayer during that time: *"Lord, let me dream the dream that YOU have for my life."* Parts of that prayer have been answered, but there are other areas that I am still waiting and standing in faith for. What we see as a setback might just be the ground the Lord is using as a setup. With every IV and each medical therapy I underwent at the clinic, I remember thinking, *God, this is hard, but make me more holy through it.* I am not huge on needles, getting blood drawn, or any type of medical procedure. To be honest, I don't like any of the above!

The grace of God that allowed me to endure those months of medical treatments is the only reason I made it through. On the first day, they told me I would have to cut out all meat for a season. I remember thinking, *I am sick and now you want me to be a vegan!?* It was challenging, but God used that short time of refraining from meat to help my body detox faster and allow the procedures to be more effective. Thankfully, I am now able to enjoy my favorite foods again (like steak!), but it required discipline to get there.

The hard can make us holy and, in my case, healthy. There are traits like perseverance and godly character that are fortified deep in us when we go through the fire. That cannot happen when everything is perfect on the mountaintop. Show me someone with a strong love for life and I guarantee you they walked through a season where they didn't know if they would have the will to live again. Show me someone with abundant joy and I imagine they had to reach a point with Jesus where the joy of the Lord became their true source of strength. This faith walk is completely opposite to the way of the world. The world wants everything to be easy so our lives will be happy and fulfilled. However, once we get to that happy place, we are never truly satisfied, so we continue the search for happiness over and over again. Happiness is fleeting, but joy remains.

The hard can make us holy and, in my case, healthy.

I believe some of the most joy-filled people I have ever met have been through some of the hardest seasons. I have a friend who is currently thriving, but there was a time when God called her to leave her homeland and move to another country with nothing but a word from God and her immediate family. She left everything behind to follow the call and will of God. She shares openly about how challenging that first year here in America was. When we met, it was her desperation for Jesus and love for KitKat bars that got her through … literally.

Sometimes the plan is not always immediately clear. There was a deeper purpose for her in that first year. She was gaining vision, clarity, and fresh dreams from God. Circumstances unfolded in ways she never would have imagined, but they were so much better because they were part of God's plan. An incredible church movement was birthed through that hard season, which I am sure she would say pruned her and her vision. I got to be part of that incredible movement. You see, our simple obedience, especially when we don't understand the "why," will not only move mountains in our own lives but will serve to benefit many others. That is authentic kingdom living.

I found that to be true in my case as well. I may never understand why I had to walk through that difficult season and, honestly, still have some health repercussions as well as protocols that I have to stay on top of. But I do know that once I was on the other side, the music project I had almost forgotten about was finally released into the world. There are songs that talk about God writing a beautiful story, how He is in the waiting, and that He is working all things together for our good. I have now lived out the truths in the songs I sing.

Your season might be painful in the present. You might want to hit delete on this chapter you are currently living. But I promise, if you allow God to use the hard, He will somehow use it to make you more holy.

Start looking at the challenges in your life as a possible part of the bigger plan. Your purpose might take on a new direction as God uses those things to help other people walk through what you did. I now know what I will never say to someone who is sick or chronically ill. I now know what I will never say to someone dealing with depression and anxiety, because I experienced some of that during my health trial. You gain invaluable wisdom, discernment, and authority when you walk through difficult trials and live to tell about it on the other side.

Take a moment now to close your eyes. I want you to picture yourself on the other side of that trial or situation you are facing. Invite God in and ask Him how to get there. Some of the best tools you have are praying, getting into the Word for God's direction, spending time in worship, and surrounding yourself with faith-filled friends who will cheer you on and not allow you to quit. Ask God to give you your own blueprint. After all, you are His daughter or son, and the Word of God says that He has plans "to give you a future and a hope" (Jer. 29:11 ESV).

Don't give up before it gets good. I promise your story is still being written. By the end of this book, I hope you'll see yourself still standing, surrendered, and your soul truly singing.

Reflection Questions

1. Is there an area in your life that feels so hard and defeating that God might be using it to bring your heart closer to Him and to forge holiness within?

2. Is there something in this "hard and holy" season that God is trying to shift in you to renew vision, get you on a new path, or reroute you in some way?

3. Is there a "hard" place in your life that you need to surrender to God?

Journal

Chapter 2

WORDS CARRY WEIGHT

Do you remember the first time you felt a little "less than" the people around you? Do you remember when you realized that perhaps life was not as perfect as you once thought?

Growing up in a nice suburban town outside of Boston, I can honestly say I was a very cheerful kid with a fantastic family life. However, my early school years brought some challenges, to say the least. By the time I was in third grade, I remember school being hard for me, not socially speaking, but I had a difficult time learning. I found myself struggling with various subjects, taking tests, and keeping up with my peers, who all seemed to be doing just fine.

One day, my third-grade teacher broke it to my parents that I had some learning disabilities, specifically with comprehension and speech. She went on to say that I was a really sweet kid with good social skills and a great personality but would not likely amount to much.

Our words carry so much weight and power in life. Our stories begin early, and it is through parents, teachers, pastors, and mentors that we begin to find our value, affirmation, and sense of significance. We've learned that children whose parents affirm, build up, and speak life over them go on to dream big, and eventually follow those dreams to even larger accomplishments and becoming giants in their fields.

However, the opposite is true for children who never had anyone speak positive affirmations into their lives. Their self-esteem, self-worth, and dreams for their lives can be quite grim. Now, as Christ followers, we know that our value, worth, and identity are rooted entirely in who He says we are. Everything else should flow out of that identity. God put us on earth with language to encourage and confirm all He says about us. When we have no one present in our lives to encourage and validate us, even in some small way, it can lead us down some dark paths. As Christians, we often forget that people need to hear positive affirmations and life-giving words from us.

We are living in a time where people are starving for truth and genuine encouragement. When we affirm and lift another person up with our words, we act as the hands and feet of Jesus to help others see themselves through the eyes of their Creator. In an age where social media is glorifying self-image and promoting self-love, it's so important to know the truth of God's Word and what He says about us. It's too easy to fall into the trap of comparison or believing the lies of what this culture deems worthy and beautiful. We must speak truth over ourselves and to one another. We must see what is shaping our value system and know why we believe what we believe.

When we affirm and lift another person up with our words, we act as the hands and feet of Jesus to help others see themselves through the eyes of their Creator.

As followers of Christ, it has to be our personal experience and relationship with God that shape this. Nobody and nothing can take that away from us. It is from this place that our identity should be formed. Every aspect of our lives then begins to flow from there. This is crucial when we look at the words we are speaking over ourselves and over others.

At some point in my third-grade year, after my teacher shared her devastating verdict, I began experiencing awful migraines. They would typically hit me later in the day, and by dinnertime, I felt so terrible that I was ready to go to bed. Thank God I was a joyful and positive kid, because it allowed me to live a normal life until they would hit. I can remember praying to God that He would take away the excruciating pain. Why am I sharing this? Because I want you to see the power that words can hold.

I want to be clear, though. I'm not saying the words that were spoken over me by my teacher made me sick. But I do want to establish that this difficult season began soon after that. There are many things that could have played into it; however, it didn't help that she predicted such a sad and dark future for me, and soon after, I was plunged into a season of sickness. Scripture speaks of the power of death and life being in our tongue (see Prov. 18:21). We can internalize emotions, and even word curses, and not know what to do with them or how to rebuke them.

Now I know to tell those words to go to the pit of hell where they belong. The more I have learned about health—emotionally, physically, and spiritually—the more I see how it is all connected. What we believe about ourselves and who God says we are will manifest in every area of our lives, which is why it is crucial to make sure you are lining up with biblical truth. Proverbs 23:7 says, "As he thinketh in his heart, so is he" (KJV). We can build up and bless, or tear down and curse, with our own words.

We can build up and bless, or tear down and curse, with our own words.

My parents were determined that the words my teacher spoke over me were not going to come to life, so much so that they began to speak words of affirmation and healing and hope over me—words that brought me life! I honestly did not know this part of my story until I was much older and doing well in school. Pretty soon those words of power would lead me to the thing that filled me with the most life, which was, and still is, music.

What Makes You Come Alive?

What is that one thing that causes you to light up? Do you know what makes you come alive? This is often the key to finding what God has called you to do. You might be naturally gifted in a specific area, or you might have to really work hard at it, but when passion and purpose collide, we often find a beautiful calling.

I remember when my childhood best friend first got a piano. I was absolutely mesmerized by it. I couldn't read music yet, but my ear began to pick out songs naturally. It got to the point where I could hear a song once and then play it back. Music drew me in time and time again, and it was one of the things, unlike certain subjects in school, that came very easily to me. This began a trend. I couldn't wait for music class and was so happy when the chorus director would put lyrics on the screen and let us sing along. The melodies drew me in and brought peace to my heart.

My parents saw my newfound interest and surprised me with a piano. I began taking lessons, which quickly became the best part of each week. My piano teacher, Mrs. Puff, was a believer in Jesus and understood the power of words. She planted seeds in my life when

I was a young child with a natural musical gift. She spoke words of encouragement and praise over me, and much like my parents, her validation helped to shape my heart. I've read studies showing that when the brains of children with learning disabilities are sparked by music, the creative side of their brains comes to life and helps them overcome those disabilities.[1] There are proven statistics on how much art and music can help children develop and learn at a faster rate.

I want to encourage anyone who may have learning issues or a specific handicap or disability, whether it be physical or mental—find that one thing that makes your heart come alive and watch what God can do in your life. Your learning limitations might not be healed, but God can and will heal your heart over time. I am so thankful this was the route God used, and that a piano, a discerning piano teacher, and incredible parents, who saw the potential in me, changed the course of my entire life.

Do you want to know the kicker to this story? I ended up graduating top of my class in high school and summa cum laude in college, and I even gave the speech at each graduation!

Allow what God says about you to be louder. Listen to the people God places in your life and what they say about you. Their words are often life giving and truth filled. Most importantly, know what the Word of God says. It is His love letter written to us. The truth of Scripture has to be our firm anchor and hope, above all other voices.

Something I often say on social media, as well as at my concerts and events, is "People do not determine your destiny. God does." I will admit that, somewhere in my journey, I became a bit of a people pleaser. Can you relate? It's so easy for us to fall into the trap of fearing man and valuing what people think more than fearing God. No one sets out to be a people pleaser. I've often seen this tendency arise when people feel deep rejection, disappointment, or even abuse early on in their lives, so they are attempting to avoid these experiences again by being overly agreeable. They typically feel a deep need to be liked and known, and to keep as many friends as possible. It can paralyze them as they desire to move forward in faith but are stuck in the "what will people think?" mode. "What if it fails, or worse, what if I fail?" is their deepest fear.

"People do not determine your destiny. God does."

Most of my life before Jesus, I focused on what I believed I was created to do, which was to sing, play piano, and write music. Like so many young hopefuls, I had dreams of becoming the next famous singer-songwriter. I look back at how fearless I was as a teenager auditioning for talent shows and singing in multiple musicals and recitals. During that time, I didn't care what anyone thought or what the outcome was because my love for it overshadowed the risk. Singing brought me life.

The only words being spoken over me at that time were from my parents and music teachers telling me "You can do it" and "You have a natural gift in this area, so go for it!" I simply believed them.

Fast-forward years after becoming a Christ follower, and now I was leading worship in church, signing a Christian record deal, recording several albums, hearing my songs on the radio (even having one #1 song on the radio), and touring in a variety of settings. It was in this season where I was asked to serve in a new capacity by pastoring people, specifically younger women and new believers. In reality, this was something I'd been doing for years while leading in various churches and small groups. Discipling others was a passion of my heart as well, but I wasn't prepared for what would have to take a temporary back seat.

The Hidden Seasons of Life

Have you ever been in a season where you felt the lies of the enemy begin to seep in through your circumstance? God still had a great plan for me, but because it wasn't packaged the way I wanted, I had to be even more on guard and able to discern the enemy's lies. This was the first time in years that I wasn't using the musical gifts and abilities that always came effortlessly. I had to face the fact that there was more to my identity than music.

As I questioned myself in this new pastoral role, a root of rejection tried to take hold in my heart. No one spoke negative words over my life or criticized me in this new position, but the enemy whispered lies to an internal wound that had been there much longer than I realized. God knew, though. He was inviting me into a hidden season in that one area where I had placed so much of my security and confidence. Because I was no longer using my musical abilities during this time, I learned that hidden seasons can produce holiness in us, if we are still and allow them to. It is in similar moments when we must examine our hearts, asking questions such as:

- Am I holding on to anything too dearly?
- Have I surrendered *everything* God has entrusted into my hands?
- Has my identity become intertwined in "what I do" instead of "who I am"?

Many of us find our identity and security in our careers, titles, relationship status, how much money we earn, or how successful we are. What words or agreements are you allowing into your soul to shape who you are, for better or for worse? If you wrestle with some of the questions above, your answers could be indicators of the areas in your heart that need freedom. Typically, these areas come out of places of deep wounding and insecurity in our lives.

The irony for me during that season was that I was still leading worship across the country at various events, and my songs continued to be played on Christian radio, so in a way, nothing had changed except my own perspective. The negative thoughts and lies weren't coming from other people but from the enemy of my soul. This experience forced me to bring every negative word or lie that I could remember, going all the way back to my childhood, to the foot of the cross, asking Jesus to show me His truth about my life.

I rejected the voice that said, "You'll never amount to much," and changed it to, "I will be all God has called and created me to be." I simply began to ask the Lord this question: "What words are *You* speaking over me?"

Are there words, statements, or lies that have been spoken over your life by other people, or by the voice of the enemy, that you need the Lord to replace with His truth? Reject every negative and ungodly belief and allow His words to hold the greatest power in your life.

Single and Still Standing

The power of God's words and truth has also been crucial in my life in the area of singleness and waiting. Let's face it, many of us who are still waiting for our "holy hotties" did not grow up thinking it would be ideal to get married and start a family in our forties or fifties. It's not the societal norm. I have to continually navigate the lies of the enemy that tell me marriage will never happen. Maybe you find yourself in the same scenario? If so, let me let you in on what I've learned in my years of waiting. It really is possible to live a full and vibrant life as a single Christian woman or man. I know it has been more common for Christian men and women to marry younger in previous generations, and I think that makes the most sense, especially when honoring God in the area of purity and waiting for marriage. But I also want to remind and encourage you that God is writing a unique and custom-made story for each one of us. He is the most creative and detailed writer of love stories and knows exactly what you need and when it's best. It will be beautiful, as long as we take our hands off the manuscript and allow Him to write it. I always say, "You will see God's hand in all areas of your life when you leave everything in God's hands."

"You will see God's hand in all areas of your life when you leave everything in God's hands."

I was twenty-one and studying jazz, pop piano, and songwriting when I first heard the gospel. I then quickly stepped into ministry and career goals with the doors God was opening for me. I fully believe the timetable of our lives will look different for each of us. To be honest, there was an extreme grace on my life in my twenties and thirties where, although I desired marriage, I didn't feel like I was missing out because I was fulfilled and living an abundant life in other areas. Yes, I was dating from time to time, but I had not met the man God had for me yet. I firmly believe and hold to the hope that my story is still being written in this area.

I will write about this topic more in the chapters ahead, but we must first reject any false words that were spoken over our lives. Maybe you have casually said things like "I will probably never see this promise fulfilled" or "I will never get married because I am too old." If you have a deep desire to be married like I do, I don't believe that our good and heavenly Father would place that in your heart without one day fulfilling it. In the same way, if you feel you're in a hard or in-between season regarding marriage, career, or another specific goal in life, He's the one who placed those desires in you for a kingdom purpose. We have to remember that His thoughts are not our thoughts, and His ways are not our ways (see Isa. 55:8).

In this season of waiting, begin declaring "No good thing will he withhold from them that walk uprightly" (Ps. 84:11 KJV) and "Delight yourself in the LORD; and He will give you the desires of your heart" (Ps. 37:4 NASB). These are truths from God's Word that carry great power. This does not mean you set the timing, but you are choosing to come in agreement with what God has already spoken.

We have the authority and power to use our words to speak life to those around us, and to speak life into unfulfilled or unrealized promises, life goals, careers, and marriages, all of which will be fulfilled in His timing, not ours.

I would love to encourage you to do a few practical things. Begin to pray into the future you believe God has for you. Write it down in a journal so you can visually look at it and refer back to it. I know the cool, new trend is to "manifest" your dreams. I don't believe we manifest anything on our own, nor would I encourage that apart from the Holy Spirit's leading. He is the only one who guides us into all truth. He will place God-ordained dreams, visions, and desires into your heart. Think on those things, visualize them, and begin praying for them. Years ago, as a new believer, I would picture myself pouring into teen girls. There was so much in my heart I longed to share with them. Things like knowing what the definition of true beauty is, where our identity comes from, and how to be secure in Christ. I would eventually go on to work with teen girls at my church for years. Did I manifest that season in my life? No. But I do believe my desire to minister to young girls was also the Lord's desire for me during that time.

Once my music career began to take off, I was invited on more and more tours. It was fun for a season, but God kept bringing me back to this vision I had of encouraging teen girls globally! Twenty-five years ago, I coined a catchy phrase and had it put on a T-shirt: "Modest is Hottest." I still believe in the message of it, although I might phrase it slightly differently now!

Instead of jumping on another music tour, I set out and began doing teen girl conferences all over the world. I would sing and speak, and encourage girls about life, purity, and choosing God's ways over the ways of the world. But if I hadn't journaled, prayed into, and served in that area as a young woman myself, I'm uncertain if that vision would have been a reality. All those years gladly pouring into teen girls locally led to a dream come true globally.

There will be areas in all our lives where the Lord is teaching us how to come into agreement with His Word, and we will gain new ground and authority in truth as we mature. The more you choose to speak life and blessing, the more authority will grow in those areas of your life, and the more you will be tested. If you feel you're being tested in one specific area, it could be that the Lord wants you to experience total freedom so you can, in turn, help others find freedom and gain new levels of authority.

You might be thinking, *So, where do I start?* Begin by searching a few verses in Scripture that correlate with what you're walking through. If the words you consistently hear are "I am ugly and flawed," then look up verses like Song of Songs 4:7: "You are altogether beautiful, my darling; there is no flaw in you." If you have trust issues and are constantly trying to figure everything out on your own, look to Proverbs 3:5–6: "Trust in the LORD with all your heart and lean not on your own understanding; in all your ways submit to him, and he will make your paths straight."

The Overflow

Have you ever sat down with a friend for coffee, and you can hear the overflow of what is really going on in their heart? You know, past the smile you can sense the hurt, offense, and fake upbeat tone despite the words that are coming out of their mouth. Deep down, you can see through every word of defeat, bitterness, discouragement, or just flat-out wanting to give up.

Maybe you find yourself in that exact same spot as you are reading this. You can hear the very words rolling off your tongue, but you know deep down you are feeling the complete opposite.

I like to call this the overflow. In Luke 6:45, it says, "The good person out of the good treasure of the heart produces good, and the evil person out of evil treasure produces evil; for it is out of the abundance of the heart that the mouth speaks" (NRSVA).

Let's look at that last part, as I am not saying you are evil in any way! "Out of the abundance of the heart the mouth speaks." We have got to tend to the soil of our hearts if we expect our words to reflect this. There are so many ways our hearts can get wounded that then affect our inner health (our spirits), which then affect our souls and what comes out of our lives and mouths. Many times we can be unaware of this until someone points it out. A few years ago, I was with a music peer who really challenged me. There is a temptation in this industry to want to "keep up with the Joneses," if you know what I mean. We were listening through several new demos of mine and on a few I would say things like "Do I sound dated?" or "Is this relevant anymore?" or "Is my voice too soft and pretty?" He looked at me very kindly and said, "I would have thought at this point in your career and with all God has done in and through your music that you would see none of that matters. You are a minister before an artist." It really struck a chord with me as I knew it was true. I began to see and hear the insecurity, fear, and disappointment that were behind those words I was speaking. I was challenged that day to begin to water the soil of my heart with the truth of God's Word and look at all He had done and was doing in my life. There was a temptation to want to fit in when God was calling me to be who He had created me to be. There were some people I needed to forgive for saying things twenty years prior out of their own opinions or feelings that were causing me to be insecure. There were some word wounds that needed to be tended. I also realized it had been several years since I went back to my original vision statement and what I felt God was asking me to do through my music ministry, artistry, etc. all those years ago and make sure I was still lining up with that vision. I think it is so important that we go back to the blueprint He has individually given to us. Not what our peers, parents, or pastors, or the powers that be may want for us, but what God has asked of us. We must also be open if He desires to change that up or invites us into a new season, holding everything openhanded and openhearted.

If we can align ourselves with who He says we are and what He is calling us to, then that will guard our hearts from so many things. Next time you are chatting with someone, begin to really listen to the words that are coming out of your mouth. Are they rooted in God's love and grace, or in fear? Is there faith or disappointment on your lips? Can you tell if some bitter waters and jealousy are coming out of the overflow of your heart and words? If so, then it is time to do a little heart work.

Reflection Questions

1. Are there any words that have been spoken over me by others that do not reflect the heart of God or line up with His truth? (If so, begin to come out of agreement with those words and speak the truth of God's Word in those areas of your life.)

2. Are there any words I am speaking about myself over my own life that do not line up with God's truth about who I am? (If so, begin to come out of agreement with those words and speak the truth of God's Word in those areas of your life.)

3. What are three words I hear God speaking over my life and the purpose He has placed on me? (Write them down and begin to pray into them.)

If you feel led, pray this prayer: *"Heavenly Father, I want to stand on Your truth. I repent of anything I have spoken over my life or have come into agreement with that was not Your truth. I ask that the blood of Jesus would cover any words or curses that have been spoken over my life. In You, I have the victory in Jesus' name. Amen."*

Journal

Chapter 3

WHEN HOPE HAS BEEN HIJACKED

Have you ever stopped to think about the changing of seasons? Every year, across many parts of the world, we experience a natural phenomenon called spring, summer, fall, and winter. Three hundred sixty-five days. Repeat. God designed nature this way on purpose. There is a distinct beauty to be found in every season, from the flowering trees at the height of springtime to the snowcapped mountains in the quiet of winter. Seasons invite us to learn more about the heart and character of our Creator. I believe the seasons we walk through in our own lives can, as well, if we are willing to lean in and listen.

Just as the seasons naturally change every few months, the seasons of our lives are never permanent. However, when we are going through a season of adversity, everything can appear dead and hopeless. It might be springtime in the natural, but inwardly you feel like you are stuck in a desert, searching frantically for a drink of water. Where are the bright blooms of the flowers that once looked alive and vibrant? Hope seems to be nothing more than memories as fleeting as the seasons. All you see ahead are dead branches and distant dreams. Have you ever felt this way? Despair so thick that you honestly couldn't fathom how you would survive the next day, or hour. I've certainly been there before. When you're in the middle of the dry desert, it's difficult to see even the smallest sign of new life. But it's there. Beneath the surface of what we see with our natural eyes, hope is there. And it wants to grow in our hearts again.

There are many references of hope throughout Scripture, but I love what John Piper says. "Biblical hope not only desires something good for the future—it expects it to happen. And it not only expects it to happen—it is confident that it will happen."[1] What happens when it becomes increasingly difficult to live in hopeful expectation, though? Proverbs 13:12 says, "Hope deferred makes the heart sick, but a longing fulfilled is a tree of life." Maybe you're holding a personal promise from the Lord that you've been waiting to come to fruition, or dreams that have simply not been realized yet. I think every person on earth has experienced seasons where hope feels as though it has been hijacked. It's not easy to navigate everyday life when we are carrying the weight of unfulfilled dreams in our hearts. But it is possible with the help and leading of the Holy Spirit. The older I get, the less I like those cheesy Christian catchphrase answers to the heartaches we all face. Yes, I trust in the Lord and His timing. Yes, I know He is working all things for my good. But I believe there are some practical steps we can take and promises we can hold fast to when we feel like hope has been hijacked.

First, where does hope come from? True biblical hope comes from God and God alone. There are many counterfeits this world promises will satisfy you, but try them temporarily, and you will find yourself quickly moving on to the next "thing" you are searching for to fill that God-shaped hope void. Only Jesus can fully sustain our hearts with hope, because He is the author and creator of it! God has placed His hope in our hearts to keep us anchored through every season. There have been times in my life where hope has come so naturally. These are typically the seasons where I am full of faith because I can see God moving in such deep and beautiful ways in my life. But what about the days when nothing in life makes sense? Prayers seem to go unheard and unanswered, and everything just feels off. Those wilderness seasons where you are fighting to regain your health, heal from a relationship that went sour, or regain control of your finances. How do we remain hopeful in the seasons of life when our faith seems smaller than even a mustard seed?

Only Jesus can fully sustain our hearts with hope, because He is the author and creator of it!

One of my favorite characters in Scripture is King David. We are told he was a "man after [God's] own heart" (1 Sam. 13:14). Not only was he a prolific songwriter (just read the book of Psalms), but he was honest and authentic, which is what I love most about his writing. He was down to earth and unafraid to express what he felt toward God. He was also far from perfect. Yet, the Lord called him a man after His own heart.

I believe heart posture isn't talked about enough in the church. We look at outward behavior and actions and are too quick to judge. Legalism runs rampant, and at times, we are completely unaware of it. We can't always see what God is doing on the inside of someone. Often, God is after the heart posture during seasons where hope seems lost.

Legalism runs rampant, and at times, we are completely unaware of it. We can't always see what God is doing on the inside of someone.

Think back to when you first encountered the love of Jesus and became a Christ follower. You experienced the salvation of God that comes through faith in Christ. I'm assuming your heart was flooded with HOPE and undeniable trust that your sins were forgiven! You were now starting a new life in Christ. The promise of eternal life most likely set your heart soaring. So ... what happened between then and now?

I have pondered this question quite a bit. It has been almost twenty-five years since I made Jesus the Lord of my life. What has caused hope to be deferred and my heart to be sick at times? Well, like many of you reading this, I have been believing and waiting on various promises from God to come to pass. Some promises MUCH longer than others! I think when we are asked to wait for longer than our flesh would prefer or when life takes a few unexpected twists and turns, hope begins to grow dim. What about when a serious trial hits your life? Perhaps the loss of a loved one, or a sickness/disease that threatens to take you out? If we are not on guard, the enemy of our soul will attempt to destroy us spiritually and remove hope from our daily vocabulary.

How does this begin? Usually with subtle lies we believe, such as "God has forgotten me" or "I'm not worthy enough so that must be why _______ has not happened yet." These are lies that the enemy knows will cause you to question and doubt the goodness and faithfulness of God. If you partner with these lies, then your lens and perspective will shift. You will fail to see the Lord as a faithful God who knows exactly what is best for your life and when to bring it about.

On the flip side, what happens when you attempt to take the reins of your life and control your own outcomes? Depression and anxiety are more likely to creep in and invade our thoughts and emotions because we are operating from a place of striving, not rest. Whenever I am tempted to control a situation or God's timing in my life, hope seems to be harder to access. Why do we continue to fall into this cycle? For me, it's because there are specific areas I struggle to surrender to God.

Patience is a fruit of the Spirit that no one enjoys growing in, but what if we viewed it as something for our good rather than something we despise? If I trust that God has *only* His best intentions and plans for my life, then why would I get anxious when my timetable doesn't line up with His? Patience cannot grow when everything is happening exactly how and when we want it to. If the goal of the Christian life is to be more like Jesus, then you better believe we are going to encounter many seasons and trials in life where this fruit must have fertile soil to grow. Something I've learned is when I grow in patience, I simultaneously grow in hope. Not the hope this world can offer, but an everlasting hope in the goodness of God no matter what my circumstances might look like. That, my friend, is true kingdom living.

If I trust that God has only *His best intentions and plans for my life, then why would I get anxious when my timetable doesn't line up with His?*

So, how do we guard our hearts against the onslaught of despair? Here are a few practical tips I try to incorporate daily that have helped me throughout the years of waiting.

Maintain an attitude of gratitude. This simple practice of starting the day by listing five things in my journal that I'm grateful for keeps my head and heart grounded. I also like to end my day thinking about what "worked" and thanking God for it. Beginning and ending my day in a posture of gratitude changes my outlook.

Let go of how you think it should look. What if we were more concerned about being obedient to the Lord than we are about societal standards? Who determines those anyway? When I read stories throughout Scripture, every person was on a unique journey with God. Your life does not have to look like the girl sitting next to you at church who got engaged in her twenties or your neighbor who is a stay-at-home mom of four little ones. It is completely unique because God created you uniquely. Begin to pray daily prayers of surrender. If there is something specific that you're holding too tightly to, then pray this simple prayer: *"God, I place this situation in Your hands and I leave it there. I only want what You want for my life. Your will alone, not mine."*

Stay present. Plan ahead when you need to, but don't get so stuck in the future that it steals your peace and hope in the present. Why not live this day to the fullest? None of us knows how many years we will have here on earth, so let's enjoy the days we do have. It's so easy to get caught up in tomorrow that we forget about the people and gifts God has placed in our lives today.

Stay anchored in the Word of God. We will all experience challenges and pain in this life. So, what anchors your heart? There are many promises in God's Word that we can cling to. We often want to cherry-pick the "feel good" verses, but what about those that refer to the Lord pruning, shaping, molding, and refining us into the people He desires us to be? Find a scripture to hold on to during your darkest days. Read it aloud and post it where you will be reminded of the truth. I have a friend who always says, "Get your face in the Book!" That is where true hope and life will arise from.

Practice forgiveness. Maybe you weren't expecting that topic in this chapter, but I think one of the quickest ways our hope can be hijacked is through unforgiveness. Anytime we take up offense toward someone, or even ourselves, we are choosing to allow bitterness to fester and grow. This can then turn into self-pity, victimhood, and despair, which are all a great recipe for hopelessness. My pastor said something profound that has always stuck with me: "Jaime, maybe you have to forgive God." I was shocked. *What!? How would I do that?* He is God, after all! Isn't that sacrilegious or something? Her point, though, was that I was disappointed in God for not allowing certain things to happen yet, and my hope in Him had shifted to a fear that He was not going to come through. Of course, God had not made any mistakes, but according to my lens, He was not coming through for me. When I released all of that to Him, I felt a tangible shift in my heart. Maybe you need to do the same. Forgiveness is the key to unlocking God's best in every area of our lives. I am not trying to make light of difficult situations or circumstances, but I do want to encourage you to not lose sight of who you are becoming through unwanted trials. I know it can be challenging to stay tethered to hope when everything seems to be unraveling. When I got sick, I felt the weight of this. I remember thinking, *Wow. My health is gone, my career is over, my home is no longer mine, and all my close friends live back in Tennessee.* Everything felt dead. I had to make a daily effort to cling to HOPE. To cling to Jesus. I would wake up in the morning with a daily debilitating headache and say out loud, "Today I choose joy. Today I choose to believe You are good. I will walk in Your hope, Lord." I won't lie, though. This didn't come easy to my flesh. I cried more tears during that season than I ever have. My circumstances didn't change overnight, but when I look back on that season, the biggest thing that changed was me. My faith, perseverance, and character grew, and most importantly, my hope in God grew. I learned that no one and no trial, sickness, or setback can do that unless you allow it to.

I had to make a daily effort to cling to HOPE. To cling to Jesus. I would wake up with a debilitating headache and say out loud, "Today I choose joy. Today I choose to believe You are good. I will walk in Your hope, Lord."

I thought about naming this book *I Surrender ALL*, because I believe the entire Christian walk is daily surrendering our will and ways to the Lord, in and through every season and situation that arises. Once my health began to improve, I realized the things I once held tightly suddenly became low on my list. Being in ministry my entire adult life, I saw how easy it was to make a platform or position an idol, or any career, for that matter. I began to see how many church workers and staff can get burned out so easily as things become a bit out of balance. This can happen in whatever field you are in. Busyness does not equal importance, but I think that message has somehow swept its way into this generation. I realized no amount of money or success will ever bring true joy, though. Joy could only be found in what I couldn't put a price on: my relationship with God and the people who stood with me through it all. This is where my hope was restored and renewed.

God has a funny way of bringing things full circle, though. I found the more I surrendered, the more doors began to open once again. My grip had loosened, and I sincerely wanted only what God had for me. Fast-forward to restored health, a new album release, going back out on tour, living back in Nashville on my own, dating again, and being nominated for a Dove Award for my *All Things* album. When I was going through everything, all of that would have been the dream of my heart. Now it was simply a sweet kiss from God and an honor to be acknowledged by my peers in my profession. But it didn't carry the weight it once would have. Why? Because I learned those temporary things, while enjoyable, will never bring true hope or joy. It was a massive career achievement, but I didn't feel anything other than immense gratitude to be alive and healthy.

I share all this to say that we serve a God who is concerned with the condition of our hearts above all else. Maybe you think that once you meet your future spouse or land your dream job, *then* everything will be right in your world. Let me say, once that dopamine and oxytocin buzz wears off, you'll be back in the same place you were before. False hope can let us down more than anything else. Have you ever lost weight, perhaps for health reasons, and then realized you still felt like the same person? That's because an outward change will never force an inward shift unless you change your thoughts and beliefs. What if we took inventory on our hearts to see if there are any areas where we are falsely placing our hope?

Our Living Hope

Hope is often used to mean "a wish: its strength is the strength of the person's desire."[2] But the biblical definition of *hope* is the confident expectation of what God has promised us for our future. If we peel things back a little bit deeper, we would begin to see that hope is actually a person. His name is Jesus, and the Bible refers to Him as our "Living Hope."

"Blessed be the God and Father of our Lord Jesus Christ! According to his great mercy, he has caused us to be born again to a living hope through the resurrection of Jesus Christ from the dead" (1 Pet. 1:3 ESV). I can remember the first time I read this verse and heard this statement. I began to think of all the things and places I had placed my hope in before I met the Lord and how unstable they could be. Careers can change in an instant, relationships can change, your health can change, your financial accounts ... basically anything on this earth could be taken away at any time. However, if our hope is rooted in the person of Jesus, that is an unshakable hope that never changes. Hebrews 13:8 says,

"Jesus Christ is the same yesterday and today and forever." This is something we can literally anchor our hearts to, firm and secure. Sure, the storms of life will still come to every single one of us, but if we hold fast to our firm foundation, then we can sail through the winds and raging seas with a hopeful heart knowing that Christ is in that boat with us at all times and will lead us to shore. There are many things this world or the enemy can try to take away from us, but did you know that HOPE is one thing they cannot? We can stand secure and steadfast in our confident hope and trust in Him no matter what we might face or what circumstances get thrown our way. This should be something we aim for as believers and is a true testament to a heart that has grown in His ways. I love how this devotional, based on 1 Peter 1:3, from Ligonier Ministries online describes hope:

> [Although there will be trials and tragedies that could] tempt [us] to succumb to belief in utter futility, both believers and non-believers know that life has an ultimate purpose. For this reason, all of humanity clings [with all they have got] to a hope of one kind or another. To lose one's hope is perhaps the most tragic thing that can ever happen in life. To say that all human beings cling to a hope, however, is not to say that all human beings have a true, living hope. Many non-believers place their hope in things that are only fleeting—money, fame, power, and so on. Yet to hope in such things

is really to be hopeless. Because such things will one day come to an end, to have hope in them is to have only a dead hope.

The Christian, however, does not have a dead hope. As Peter tells us ..., we have a living hope.... This living hope will never end and sustains us as we endure suffering.

Ours is a living hope only because its foundation is the resurrection of Jesus from the dead (v. 3). The fact that Jesus was raised to life two thousand years ago gives us an unshakable conviction that our hope is not in vain. His resurrection vindicates Him as the Lord of creation who is even now making all things new (Rev. 21:5).

This living hope is our hope of salvation.... The new life that we have in Christ is something that can never be taken away. In fact, it will be even more glorious once we reach the eternal state.[3]

We can stand secure and steadfast in our confident hope and trust in Him no matter what we might face or what circumstances get thrown our way.

I want to invite you to take a moment to pause and then ask yourself two simple questions:

1. Where does my hope come from?
2. Has my hope been hijacked?

However you may have answered, the best remedy to renewing your hope is to renew your heart before Jesus. Just like King David, you may have to really have it out. I love the psalm that says, "Pour out your hearts before Him; God is a refuge for us" (62:8 NASB). What is holding you back? Pour it all out and then ask the Holy Spirit to fill you fresh with the love and hope of Jesus. Ask for His divine guidance and perspective for whatever you might be walking through. If you do not know the Lord or have not asked Him into your life, I encourage you to start there. Recognize that you are in need of a Savior. The Bible says, "For all have sinned and fall short of the glory of God" (Rom. 3:23). Admit your sins to Him and ask for forgiveness and then turn from them. Invite Jesus to be the Lord of your life. Get a Bible and begin studying who this Jesus is. Find a good local church and someone who can disciple and mentor you. This will be the very best decision you will ever make, and this will begin your journey of knowing the true and living hope, Jesus.

I won't promise everything will change in a moment, but I do believe the Lord will pursue your heart to a place of surrendered hope. Or if you have been walking with Him for years, allow Him to freshly woo your heart back to that place of hope. My legs have gotten wobbly throughout many seasons of a hope deficiency, but I can also confidently say I am still clinging to Him with all I have got and with a hope that's no longer being hijacked.

Journal

Chapter 4

GOD'S TIMETABLE IS ON TIME

Raise your hand if you've ever noticed God's timetable is a little different from yours. Raising two hands high over here! The Bible says that "with the Lord a day is like a thousand years, and a thousand years are like a day" (2 Pet. 3:8). That can be difficult for our finite minds to comprehend. I don't know about you, but I've definitely lived days that felt as though they lasted a thousand years. The crazy thing is, though, a thousand years is still short to God.

The New Testament uses the word *kairos* to refer to God's timing. It means "the appointed time in the purpose of God" or "the time when God acts." For example, in Mark 1:15 it says, "the *kairos* is fulfilled, and the kingdom of God is at hand" (ESV).[1]

There are those who say God's timing is perfect because He exists on a different wavelength and has a supernatural view of time. We may never fully understand from this side of heaven. But the longer I'm on this faith journey with Jesus, I can't help but notice that the things we understand least are the very things God knows we need most. God's timing is always better than ours. I'll admit that it doesn't always feel that way in the moment, but there is no denying His goodness when I look back on my life and see His faithfulness woven throughout. I still have dreams and promises I'm trusting God for, but even in the midst of the unknowns, I can wait with anticipation knowing God will come through because His track record is proven: He *always* keeps His promises. When we choose to lean into Him instead of wrestling with what we don't understand, His incomparable peace will guide us down the path He designed specifically for us. This all sounds really beautiful, and it truly is! But here's the thing ... I'm overwhelmingly human. I'd be lying if I said I haven't tried to force my own way or push something to happen in my own timing. You too? I'm glad I'm not alone! That means we can embark on this faith journey together and trust that God's plans for us really are as good as He says. (Spoiler alert: They are!)

God's timing is always better than ours.

Have you ever found yourself praying without end and still not seeing any change in your circumstances? It's easy to spiral into a million anxious thoughts wondering how your life is happening at a pace so different from the one you imagined. I've been there many times. The societal expectations only make it worse when I'm already feeling the disappointment of missing the boat while everyone else is sailing away to their happily ever after.

I always imagined my life would follow the typical timeline: go to college, land my dream career, get married to my husband, and have a house filled with a few kids ... all by my thirtieth birthday. But as it turns out, the tailor-made story God is writing over my life looks nothing like that picture. There's not a white picket fence or a handsome prince riding in on a white horse, and yet, even here in the unknown and continued waiting, I know I haven't missed out on God's best for my life. My confidence doesn't rest in what I can see around me but in the promises of the God who dwells inside of me. I truly believe we can rest assured that we are right on time if we are walking in obedience to the Lord and what He has asked of each of us personally. Waiting, on its own, isn't enough though; we must learn to wait well and make decisions that prepare us for what we're praying for. We can delay the process when we're walking in disobedience or remaining stuck in a sin pattern. Remember, God's ways are higher and better, but that doesn't necessarily mean they'll always feel easier or more preferable. Sometimes life just happens: the car breaks down, you lose a job, your health suddenly declines, or a relationship ends. It may feel like you're going backward when life hits hard, but oftentimes it is those very circumstances that confirm you're heading in the right direction. Jesus said that we will face trials here on earth, but it's the promise afterward that changes everything. We take heart because He has overcome the world (see John 16:33). How insignificant our problems become when we look to Him who has overcome it all and, even more, can use our trials for our greater good and His ultimate glory. Only God could do that! Aren't you thankful?

Maybe you don't find yourself in a place of overwhelming gratitude today. You may feel like a broken record asking God for the same thing over and over again. I'll be the first to admit I have grown weary of pressing in to pray while not seeing anything shift in the natural. After waiting over twenty years for prayers to be fulfilled, it's tempting to just throw in the towel and stop asking altogether. Defeat and discouragement have often tried to take root in the soil of my soul, but all that ever grows from that place is bitterness and resentment, which is not good ground for waiting well. I've found myself in a place of total defeat where I cynically began to take no action whatsoever but, instead, left it up to God. That may sound like the right course of action, but it wasn't from a place of unwavering and deep trust. It matters how we wait on God. Our thoughts matter. Our heart posture matters. This is where we "faith it till we make it," as I like to say. Where we act on what we don't feel or see—believing that God will ultimately come through for us.

This is where we "faith it till we make it," as I like to say. Where we act on what we don't feel or see—believing that God will ultimately come through for us.

Faith in the Timing

Looking back, few seasons of my life have required more faith than when I suddenly had to surrender my home when I was ill, as I mentioned earlier. I absolutely loved everything about that condo: the way light pierced through the high ceilings and highlighted the beautiful interiors and furniture I had worked hard to design and pick out. Home had never felt sweeter, and because it was a brand-new unit, I never imagined that I'd soon be packing it all away due to unforeseen mold. This is a huge ordeal for anyone, but it was especially challenging as I was battling Lyme disease. Mold illness goes hand in hand with Lyme disease, and for whatever reason, most people who battle Lyme have significant issues with mold as well. I'll never forget how crushing it felt to hear that mold toxicity kept showing up in my blood work. It was at that very moment I had to decide to do the hard and holy thing by selling my dream home. This decision ultimately led me to relocating back to Nashville, where I lived twenty years prior, and I found myself renting a room in a friend's beautiful home. I knew this was a temporary move but had absolutely no idea what the next steps would look like. The market in Tennessee was incredibly wild due to the pandemic, so it was not an ideal time to buy a home. If I'm being honest, it felt as though I was beginning to move backward in the timetable of my life. Going from owning to renting felt like settling… and I don't mean settling into my dream home. God's ways are so obviously different from ours, but they are also better, even when our emotions tell us otherwise. Isaiah 55:8–9 says, "'For my thoughts are not your thoughts, neither are your ways my ways,' declares the LORD. 'As the heavens are higher than the earth, so are my ways higher than your ways and my thoughts than your thoughts.'"

My thoughts often went back to years prior when I was working at a church, and I had the most beautiful commute. I would drive past a neighborhood full of brand-new builds that were perched in a location I could only dream of living in. Any Hallmark movie fans here? This neighborhood looked like a picturesque scene straight out of Hallmark. I'm a bit of a hopeful romantic and am drawn to anything that is eye catching and beautiful. If things had gone my way, you'd catch me rolling up to one of those perfectly manicured homes. Instead, God's way led to that cozy little room in a friend's home. Sharing a bathroom took some adjusting on my part, but trying to bond with her dog took even more flexibility, especially considering he liked to break off the leash when I'd try to walk him. I share all this to remind you that oftentimes what seems like a set-back is actually a setup for God to show up and show off for us. In those uncomfortable moments, He was refining my character and preparing me for the deepest desires of my heart to come to fruition. God is much more interested in growing our character than making us comfortable. It's easy to feel blindsided when things don't go our way, but if our ultimate goal in this life is to be more like Jesus, then we shouldn't be shocked when He shakes our world and asks us to surrender to His best.

God is much more interested in growing our character than making us comfortable.

Divine Timing

Have you ever had a kairos moment where you knew without a doubt that God was at work? We know He is always moving on our behalf and for our good, but there are times when we need eyes of faith to really push past what we see in the natural. Several years had passed since I first drove past that finished and beautiful spot, and much to my surprise, a couple of friends who just moved into a unit asked me to house-sit for them. It was the most peaceful weekend getaway, and I just couldn't shake the feeling in my spirit that I would live there one day, even though I couldn't wrap my mind around how. I had just finished a sabbatical season and wasn't working much since healing was my main priority. This all led to a divine connection with a couple visiting from Colorado. I assumed my friends knew them already, but as it turned out, we were all meeting for the first time.

Have you ever felt like you were meant to meet certain people for a much larger purpose? These were kingdom-minded people with the biggest hearts, and my spirit connected with them even though I had no clue why. Several weeks later, I ended up in the courtyard of that same beautiful complex to record a podcast interview, and who walked up right as I was walking out? Yep, you guessed it ... that same incredible couple. We conversed again and exchanged phone numbers as this God connection I felt continued to intensify. It felt as though I had known them for years, because we were linked by the Spirit of God and our love for Him.

The timing was interesting since I was at a crossroads with deciding whether to stay in Nashville or return to my New England home. To rent or to buy, that was the question. But where and how? This is where God's ways enter. Little did I know, those courtyard conversations would soon turn into a divine connection that would lead me to living in that dream complex alongside those incredible people God handpicked to place in my life. They have been a reflection of God's love and care for me, and I'm forever grateful for the connection we share with one another. I share all this to remind you that there is a huge difference between natural timing and divine timing. None of this would have ever happened if I hadn't found myself uprooted from my comfortable condo. I could have forged my own way and purchased a home in a declining economy, but instead, I followed God's voice and found myself surrounded by relationships fueled by a mutual desire to live for kingdom purposes above our own. Frustration and fear can lead us to manipulate the timing of when we think things should happen, but I can tell you with full confidence that I've never lost anything by leaving everything in God's hands. I want to invite you to take a moment to pause and bring these questions before the Lord:

"God, is there something You are asking me to surrender to You in regard to Your timing?"

"Is there any area of my life where I am trying to make things happen or hustle my way into that answered prayer instead of resting in You?"

There Is a Time for Everything

A critical part of this walk with Jesus is becoming acquainted with the times and seasons. One of my favorite passages of Scripture is Ecclesiastes 3:1–8, and it says:

> There is a time for everything,
> and a season for every activity under the heavens:
> a time to be born and a time to die,
> a time to plant and a time to uproot,
> a time to kill and a time to heal,
> a time to tear down and a time to build,
> a time to weep and a time to laugh,
> a time to mourn and a time to dance,
> a time to scatter stones and a time to gather them,
> a time to embrace and a time to refrain from embracing,
> a time to search and a time to give up,
> a time to keep and a time to throw away,

> a time to tear and a time to mend,
> a time to be silent and a time to speak,
> a time to love and a time to hate,
> a time for war and a time for peace.

With so many things vying for our time and attention, it is crucial that we intentionally set our eyes and affection toward Jesus. It is there, and there alone, where we learn to fall in step with the Holy Spirit and the ways He is guiding and leading our every decision. We live in a hustle culture where being busy is equated to being important, successful, popular, and well-connected. With social media and streaming services replacing real-life connections, distractions are at an all-time high. If there really is a time for everything, then how do we make the time to intentionally sit at the feet of Jesus?

As a trained pianist, I remember my lessons were centered around timing. Music is full of different cadences, just as we find throughout our own lives. Our days naturally ebb and flow, much like a song does. There are times when God will ask us to slow down, but if our hearts are not in the right place, it may feel like He is holding us back from what we long for the most. It's natural to fight against the urge to be still, but it's in the still and quiet where we realize our God-given purpose and identity. God slows us down in order to heal our hearts and minds from what could hinder us from the future He has planned. If you find yourself in a season where God is asking you to slow down, lean in and trust Him. Yield to it. Pushing through isn't the answer. He invites us to rest in Him as He fulfills His promises in the timing He knows is best.

God invites us to rest in Him as He fulfills His promises in the timing He knows is best.

Early in my career, I struggled with boundaries. I had a hit song on the radio, and as a result, tour dates were flooding in left and right. It felt like I had no choice but to say yes to everything. However, I quickly learned the hard way that boundaries were a necessity. I was new to full-time ministry and had no clue that self-care wasn't selfish; it was actually vital if I wanted to have anything of substance to pour into others. Finding that cadence in life is crucial. I often think about how Jesus regularly withdrew from people and crowds to sit in solitude. How much more do we need to take that time and follow in our Savior's footsteps?

Maybe you find yourself in a full-on season right now where the very thought of rest seems unreachable. How are we expected to slow down when our careers, our relationships, and the demands of life are all competing for our time and attention? In music, we call it an *accelerando*. It means a tempo that is "gradually increasing in speed."[2] When we walk step by step with God, we are able to settle in and out of the paces each season holds. As you trust God for His timing in your life, would you take a moment to pause and ask Him if you are in His rhythm for your life, or your own? Are you speeding up or slowing down? Are you running your race at the pace God has for you? Ask Him to search your heart as you ponder these questions.

At the end of Ecclesiastes 3, the writer goes on to say, "He has made everything beautiful in its time. He has also set eternity in the human heart; yet no one can fathom what God has done from beginning to end" (v. 11). Wow, those are some powerful words! You know what part always gets me? That no one, absolutely no one, can fathom what God has done. There's so much mystery surrounding our walk with Jesus, which is exactly why it's called a life of faith. There would be nothing to pray about or hope for if we knew all the details ahead of time. The most detrimental part of that would be missing out on a full relationship with our Savior. Our questions lead us toward Him and take us deeper than easy answers ever could. As we wait, God is building our trust muscles and making our faith stronger day by day. If it's not good yet, then He's not done yet. So, we wait expectantly for His promises to unfold. It's tempting to fall into self-pity, doubt, and insecurity while we are waiting, but as we intentionally choose to seek life in the barren places, God is actively lining up what we can't see and putting the pieces of the puzzle together in a way we could never imagine. Instead of looking at the things we do not have or are still believing for, we can embrace all that we do have in Him.

Instead of looking at the things we do not have or are still believing for, we can embrace all that we do have in God.

I have always believed there is a difference between desperately waiting versus confidently waiting. As believers, our confidence comes from the truth of God's Word and not from our own understanding. I am so thankful for the Bible and all the scriptures that point me to my eternal hope! His words have become lifelines for me as I continue to brave the waters of walking by faith in Jesus.

His Timing Is Trustworthy

Have you ever struggled with trust issues? I hear this question asked many times when I'm with friends who are dating, or even my friends who are married. For some of us, our hearts are so prone to suspicion, which often stems from past wounds of hurt, rejection, and the traumas of life we've faced. Maybe you were deeply hurt in a romantic relationship or in a friendship, or perhaps even by a pastor or a parent. That pain is real and I'm so sorry you've walked through that. If we are not careful, though, we can easily build up walls around our hearts and not live in a space where we believe the best of people or trust what they say is true, which makes it difficult to open our hearts to those who God places in our lives. There is a time and place for wisdom and discernment, but I also see wounded, rejected believers convinced they are being discerning when, in reality, they are carrying hurt, offense, jealousy, and past wounds that have not been brought to the foot of the cross for healing. That sentence may have poked the corners of your heart a bit, and that's okay. I've had to work hard in this area after a relationship went sour and my trust was deeply broken. This created an overflow of emotions that caused me to expect those who came into my life to behave in the same way others in the past had. It wasn't until I dealt with that wound that I experienced freedom from judging others based on what I perceived to be true. Healing the heart matters in the timeline of our lives. No one is exempt from this need of restoration, not even those you'd consider to be the godliest people. We all fall short, and we all need redemption. Jesus was sinless, pure, kind, gentle, strong, meek, and perfect in character. That is why we can trust Him. If you have given Him your heart, then you have been washed in His cleansing blood and made new, but we are still human and we still need Him. We have flaws and weaknesses, and will continue to make mistakes as we press forward in this good fight. Thank God for His gift of forgiveness and salvation! I realized that if I really say I trust God with my whole heart and life, then I must trust His timing as well. You cannot have one without the other.

I realized that if I really say I trust God with my whole heart and life, then I must trust His timing as well. You cannot have one without the other.

Below is a list of many of the attributes of who God says He is. Let these eleven words about who God is wash over you. There are so many more, but I thought this was a great place to start. Take each one and write down any you may have a hard time believing. Write out every root of doubt in your heart and mind that might appear around the corresponding attribute of God. Ask Him to show you who He is to you. He IS:

- Protector
- Provider
- Deliverer
- Healer
- Comforter
- Savior
- Restorer
- Redeemer
- Faithful
- Merciful
- Kind

Each one of these fully embodies the character of God! Read it until you believe it, and then read it again and again.

Journal

Chapter 5

WHEN YOUR PLAN B IS GOD'S PLAN A

There are certain areas of our lives that are going to happen at a specific stage, age, or time frame, and it will look different for everyone. I am one of those people with crazy faith who believe that if God desires you to get pregnant when you're fifty, then He can and will make it happen. I also understand there are very real factors that affect all this, so before I jump in, please hear my heart. I realize this can be a sensitive subject for both men and women, so I want to lay this out as carefully as I can. I have had countless conversations with the Lord about waiting and trusting His timing, especially because of how He designed the female body to bear children. God sees beyond what we are able to see, however, and He does not hold out on what's best for His children, even when we may feel that our biological clock is running out of time. What feels like plan B to us has actually been His plan A all along. Maybe you've had a longing in your heart to be a parent for as long as you can remember. For others, the pain of a miscarriage may linger on as you continue to try again and again for that beautiful rainbow child. I have certainly found myself with a similar longing to be a mother, offering up my desires to the Lord in true surrender, trusting that His plan is best even when I don't understand it in the least.

During a specific season in my life, I had just finished a grueling tour and was not in the best headspace. This is what I call the "post-tour blues." I was in my late thirties at the time and had been on the road with some wonderful artists and speakers, all of whom quickly became like a little family to me. We had experienced some incredible events where we strongly sensed the Holy Spirit moving every night, from city to city and venue to venue. I recall a conversation I had after one of our last shows when a sweet older woman approached my resource table and shared her beautiful story of God's faithfulness. She had married much later in life and went on to have children of her own, experiencing the joys of family life in full. My heart was flooded with hope in that moment, and I couldn't help but ask her how old was "older." Any guesses? Well, lower them. She shared that she got married at thirty-five and was pregnant with her first child by thirty-six. I knew she meant well, and I have certainly experienced much worse conversations after many years on the road, but this one still stung a little. I suddenly felt that bubble of hope burst as the number thirty-five left her mouth. That revelation was quickly followed by "You must be about thirty, right?" Don't get me wrong, I love that I look younger than I am (thank You, Lord, for good genes and a healthy lifestyle!), but if I'm being honest, I was still really bummed over that conversation. When I got back from the tour, I kept thinking about our interaction and what God might have me glean from it. I was physically spent, emotionally drained, and in desperate need of some time off to rest and get refilled. It definitely takes me a few days to recenter and recover after being on the road for so long. I wish I could remember the exact details of this next part, but I decided to book either a massage or a facial for some self-care and relaxation in the days following. What I do remember is that the spa employee was extra chatty while all I wanted was a little peace and quiet. During my session, she asked me two common questions everyone loves to ask: *"Are you married?"* and *"How many children do you have?"* I'm sure it was a combination of the post-tour blues and where I was at in my cycle, but my typical Jesus-loving, kind response did not come out of my heart or my mouth. Instead, I said something along the lines of "No, I'm not married, and I pray my eggs are not drying up" in a very snippy tone. I think I might have shed a tear or two as well. Don't worry, I gave her a big tip at the end because I felt guilty for snapping at her.

Here's the thing: Each of us has something we are waiting on. We are all currently living in the in-between. We also all have that one thing that will trigger our hearts and reveal a place that the Lord longs to bring inner healing to. My prayer is that you'll walk away with encouragement and practical tools from these pages to help you navigate your waiting season with joy. Of course, there will be times when people, circumstances, and life in general will hit that tender spot in your heart, and your responses to others may show you where you need healing the most. Pay attention to when that happens instead of brushing it away.

I knew I needed to take time to give this place in my heart and my desires back to the Lord. For a while, I was coasting on ministry and career dreams coming to pass, and I loved it. There is nothing wrong with that, either. God creates full lives in some of the emptiest of places on purpose. I can honestly say that I am living an abundant life, even while I'm hanging out in the waiting room. But without the daily or weekly talks with God about the areas I'm still waiting on, all I was doing was ignoring the reality that, oftentimes, things in life do not always happen when and how we want them to. So, I got real and asked Him the hard questions.

> *"God, why am I not married?"*
> *"Lord, will I ever have children of my own?"*

Sure, I go on dates and setups, and I have certainly had past relationships, but even so, I've not yet found my missing puzzle piece. I wish I could tell you that I heard the audible voice of God giving me His blueprint and master plan for this area of my life, but instead, I heard Him begin to remind me of so many truths from HIS WORD. This is where we should go first for direction and guidance. I am all for motivational messages, incredible sermons, prophetic words, and encouragement from friends and family, but at the end of the day, it is the Word of God that we need to be anchored in. His promises, His ways, and His truth. I am so thankful that we do have a blueprint: the Bible.

I remember being led to Psalm 139 and the sweet reassurance of how God made me and sees me. His Word reminds me there is nothing wrong with me, and that, in fact, He knit me together in my mother's womb. He says that "I am fearfully and wonderfully made" (v. 14). His thoughts and words are what mean the most. Every single detail about your heart and mind has been held in God's hands. He knows the deepest desires of our hearts because He formed and fashioned them at the beginning of time, so He also knows His best for each of us. Around this same time when God was reassuring me, He began talking to me about His plans for my life, and how many of the dreams He placed in my heart had to happen first. I wasn't failing in any area, and to be honest, there were several instances where I could have easily made it happen outside the will of God, if I really wanted to. Instead, I was doing my best to walk in obedience and wholeheartedly believe that God honored that. In 1 Samuel 15:22 it says, "To obey is better than sacrifice." I cannot tell you how many times I've had to choose God's best and highest plans over the systems and ways of this world. I know to nonbelievers we may appear crazy, but I have never once regretted being obedient to His voice.

Not too long after this, I had a huge revelation while on a sunset walk. No matter the season I'm in, I like to do things with my entire heart. I am either all in on assignment from the Lord or all out. As I was walking, I realized I would not have been able to travel in ministry while also being the kind of wife and mother I so desperately long to be. My heart would have been constantly conflicted. I do not say any of this to shame working mothers who are traveling in some capacity. God calls each of us down different paths, and He knows how to best sustain us. I couldn't help but feel thankful and full of deep gratitude as I remembered God is always right on time. He knows when I'll be ready, and I find rest and peace in that truth.

Above and Beyond

As many of you may already know, fertility rates have dropped to alarmingly low percentages in the last several years. I am not a doctor, but I love to study holistic health practices and biohacking, much of this stemming from my journey of battling and overcoming Lyme disease. Maybe you are suffering with a physical or mental health situation as well. There are many new ways to treat health issues that aren't typically discussed during a quick visit to the doctor. Even simple things like healthy sleep, the quality of water you drink, food sourcing, and adequate sunlight and movement can be life altering for someone who is battling a chronic health condition. If your doctor is not trying to get to the root cause, then you may want to investigate integrative or functional medicine to see about getting relief while making natural lifestyle changes. So much of the fertility decline can be attributed to the environmental toxins we are now exposed to compared to when our parents were having children. Unfortunately, our food supply is filled with many pesticides, our water sourcing is no longer pure, and the number of endocrine disrupters in our personal products, makeup, perfume, and detergents is at an all-time high, which, in turn, is wreaking havoc in our reproductive and endocrine systems. Factor in the busy lifestyle most have, plus the amount of stress people are under, and it really adds up quickly. Now, I know I am one of those people who are completely all in when it comes to a healthy, holistic lifestyle, but I also know it can become an idol, just as anything else in our lives can. I choose to live a certain way to keep my body working as best as possible, especially after walking through a chronic disease. But we also have to remember that some things are out of our control.

Let me tell you the story of a dear friend I really admire. My friend Lynette always wanted a family. She was in full-time ministry, was killing it in her business career, and eventually got married at the age of forty-two. She also became mom to four bonus boys, as she likes to say. She and her husband started trying for children, and she got pregnant a few years later but, sadly, miscarried soon after. As you can imagine, she was devastated but continued to cling to the promises of God in the midst of her pain. Soon after, they walked through a season where they suddenly and gut-wrenchingly lost their son to cancer at the young age of twenty-three. They were full of devastation and grief, and Lynette began to give up on her dream of having any more children. One thing I love about God is that He never gives up even when we may choose to. He is always working behind the scenes on our behalf and lining things up that we have no idea about. Doubt, disappointment, and hope deferred can leave us forgetting dreams and desires, but God does not forget them for even a moment. If He created our hearts, then He knows the most intimate details of them. Why would a good God put a deep desire there and not fulfill it?

One Christmas morning, Lynette and Ron received a call that a woman who knew them through a friend had just given birth, and they were the only couple she wanted to raise her baby. Shortly after that call, two twin baby girls were placed in their arms, who they ended up adopting. Talk about a Christmas miracle! I watched Lynette go from barren to holding not one but two precious baby girls, who just so happen to look exactly like her and Ron. Lynette would tell you everything has felt right on time, and the only explanation for that is the grace of God. She was fifty-two years old when that call came.

As we wait on the Lord, our needs are met as they come, and we eventually see that His ways truly are higher and better than our own. Perhaps where you're at now is not your plan A, but you can rest assured it was always God's. When you give your heart to Christ, you are surrendering your life for the life He has planned. It's so easy to say things like "not my will, but Your will be done" and then instantly forget that when something doesn't go our way. It takes faith, courage, and true surrender to live for Jesus, but it is always, always worth it.

Instant Obedience

I'm sure you have heard the phrase "Delayed obedience is disobedience." I remember the first time I heard it. I was a new believer and was still in the beginning stages of working out many areas in my heart and life. I was in a friendship-turned-romantic relationship with this guy who I thought was so dreamy. Plus, he even loved the Lord! Although it started out very pure, there came a point when I knew we were in deep, murky waters.

Have you ever been there? You sense the conviction of the Holy Spirit guiding and leading you away from the temptation and then ... bam! The flesh is the flesh and can be very weak. I have this word I use with a close friend, and it's called being "fleshy." We can call it out quickly when we see it on full display in one another because it's that noticeable. Now that is a good friend! Iron truly does sharpen iron, so make sure you have people in your life who not only tell you how great you are and cheer you on but also challenge you to grow in your relationship with Christ and do the deeper and harder heart work.

The Bible is super clear that we are to walk in the Spirit and not in the flesh. "So I say, walk by the Spirit, and you will not gratify the desires of the flesh. For the flesh desires what is contrary to the Spirit, and the Spirit what is contrary to the flesh. They are in conflict with each other, so that you are not to do whatever you want" (Gal. 5:16–17). As we know, this is not always an overnight transformation. We all have various strongholds and patterns that we need to break free from in Christ. One day in particular, I sensed that I needed to talk with someone about this relationship and seek godly counsel and advice. This was the first relationship I had been in as a Christ follower, and my heart genuinely wanted to do things in a way that honored God. Instead of instant obedience, I delayed that conversation because I knew deep down in my heart the relationship was not right, and they would encourage me to lay it down.

Well, let me tell you, things went from muddy waters to the whole swamp really quick. I often look back, twenty-plus years later, and wonder why I didn't instantly obey, and I can't help but wonder what my path would have looked like if I had. I can say with certainty there would have been much less heartache, confusion, and a less prolonged wrong season.

God is so kind when we come to Him and repent, and He puts us right back on track. There are consequences to our sinful ways, though. I think one of the reasons we delay obedience is that we get comfortable doing things the way we want to, or we become blinded by the false illusion that we can somehow control a situation. Sometimes the broken areas of our hearts hold on to things for our own comfort and protection, even when it is not what is best for us. I am learning more and more that when I feel the slightest nudge to do, or not do, something, I must obey instantly without any hesitation. I don't want delayed obedience to result in even further delays or detours that the Lord never planned. You see, I believe it is out of His rich love for us, and the fact that Jesus walked this earthly road and knows what temptation, suffering, and attacks of the enemy are like, that He has so much compassion for us. He truly takes our plans, even the ones that were never part of His, and somehow works it all together for our good. It was soon after I finally ended that relationship that God opened a big door in ministry: I signed my first record deal. He longs to be gracious to us, and His kindness leads us to repentance, so why do we still delay obedience at times? I have some questions at the end of this chapter that might help.

Sometimes the broken areas of our hearts hold on to things for our own comfort and protection, even when it is not what is best for us.

There Is More Than Enough

After walking with Jesus for nearly twenty-eight years, I have seen a thing or two. There are times when we can live out of a scarcity mindset instead of a "God's got more than enough for all of us" kind of mindset. In Psalm 34:10 we are told, "Those who trust in the LORD will lack no good thing" (NLT).

Do you battle with comparison, constantly thinking someone else's life is better than yours? Maybe you look at their clothes, home, or family and think, *Wow! It's all so beautiful.* But deep down, do you wish you had what they have? Or maybe it is directed toward a season of life that you wish you were in. You are outwardly happy for someone when they are in a winning season, yet inside you're thinking, *When is it going to be my turn?* I do think it's important to be honest with ourselves about where we are. I have seen multiple friendships go south under the guise of a "misunderstanding" when, in reality, one of the parties involved felt left out. I wish we would address this more in the church. If I had a giant megaphone, I would say at the top of my lungs, "THERE IS MORE THAN ENOUGH WITH GOD!" He has unlimited resources and more than enough ways to make things happen in our lives. Just because you were not invited somewhere or included in something does not mean He cannot open a door somewhere else. God is protecting us from things that we think are best. I always say, "Man's rejection is God's redirection." Just because you did not end up with the guy *you* thought would be best does not mean that God is withholding marriage from you. Just because you were not welcomed into that event, ministry, dream job, or friendship does not mean that God overlooked you. Maybe He did not want you there for a reason. Trust the nos and the divine delays. There is always a bigger purpose in them. We operate out of a scarcity mentality when we have not dealt with deeper wounds. Perhaps you were treated poorly by a parent, teacher, or church. Subconsciously you begin to operate out of that pain and automatically assume people are not showing up for you the way you want. That is a wonderful time to do a heart check. Our emotions are valid; however, there are times when we are stuck in patterns that are not Christlike, which require God's healing in our hearts. Comparison, envy, jealousy, and choosing to have a critical spirit toward people are never God's best for us.

"Man's rejection is God's redirection."

If we are honest with ourselves, many times these feelings are rooted in our own insecurities because we still need a revelation of our identity in Christ. Do you know that God commands us to "love your neighbor as yourself" (Lev. 19:18 MSG)? If God is crazy about you and in love with you, then you can like who you are and can even learn to love yourself. For years I thought it was selfish to love myself or make sure I was taking care of my own needs. I am not talking about some sort of self-centered "me, myself, and I" type of life. But God does want us to take care of our own hearts, bodies, and minds so we are better equipped to serve and love others.

At times, it can also come down to a control issue. We have to be able to relinquish all control and trust that, while we see in part, God sees in full. Don't forget that this lifetime here on earth is just the beginning of forever in eternity with Him. There will be things in all of our lives that simply make no sense on this side of heaven. Are you holding tightly to what you want instead of living completely surrendered and openhanded to the One who created you? Would you take a minute to reflect and ask these questions to yourself:

1. Am I holding on to a plan for my life that might not be God's plan?
2. Am I open to my life looking completely different from what I thought it would?

I want you to do something. Take out a journal or something to speak into. You might feel awkward at first, but would you start to write down or talk out every plan or dream that you currently have? Have the freedom to be as detailed as you can and then listen to or read it back. What is your plan A? After you have done this, I want you to pray this: *"Holy Spirit, is there anything You want me to edit, change, or surrender?"* See what He says. Maybe He will give you a new direction in an area, or perhaps He will say, "That guy or gal you have been holding on to in your heart the last few years? Yeah, I need you to fully surrender it like it is not happening." Are you willing and open to doing that? He may show you that you need to seek restoration in a relationship or that it's time to start looking for a new job. There are plans we have that the Lord may be wanting to alter. What I love is that He is gracious and will gently lead us into His path for our lives. Don't trade God's timing for your deadline. He does not have expiration dates when His plans are involved.

Journal

Chapter 6

THE THOUGHTS WE THINK

Have you ever taken inventory of all the thoughts that pass through your mind in just one day? I call it "the thought test," which is basically the sum of all the things I am thinking about and dwelling on. I ask myself, *Is my thought life full of what is true, noble, pure, and praiseworthy? Or are my thoughts destructive, negative, and in opposition to the words my heavenly Father would be speaking over me?* We're instructed in this way in the book of Philippians 4:8, which says, "Finally, brothers and sisters, whatever is true, whatever is noble, whatever is right, whatever is pure, whatever is lovely, whatever is admirable—if anything is excellent or praiseworthy—think about such things."

I recently went on a beach vacation with a friend who asked me a question that quite honestly caught me off guard. She said, "Do you realize the negative self-talk you keep falling into in that one area of your life?" That question totally hit home because I knew she was absolutely right. Somewhere within the last six months, I had begun to partner with negative, limiting beliefs about myself. The beach was the perfect place to exacerbate these thoughts, as I slipped into a swimsuit that was fitting a bit different from the summer before. When I took a step back and really looked at the situation, I could see the plan of the enemy and how cunning he was in convincing me to believe that I was not enough as I walked through difficult circumstances out of my control.

Have you ever been there? The lies just became louder. *If you were only thinner or had worked out more, then you would feel better in this swimsuit and would be carelessly frolicking around in the sand.* Sure, there was some truth to this. I had stopped working out for several months while trying to overcome chronic fatigue and a foot injury that had reared its ugly head. But the bigger truth is I should feel good about who I am, know my value, and be free on the beach no matter what size I am. So, I began to renew my mind on that trip. The way I did this was by showing myself the same compassion and love I would to a friend. I thanked my body for getting through a new album release and three months of nonstop touring, all while making the best food choices I could while on the road. I was also navigating deep relational heartache throughout that time and decided I needed to give myself the same love and hope I so freely offered to others.

Why do we beat ourselves up so dang hard? I honestly believe it is deeply rooted in our thoughts and ungodly beliefs, and this is something I had to intentionally navigate while suffering with a chronic illness. We each have the choice to either come under our thoughts or rise above them, and while it is true that the thoughts we carry about ourselves matter, so do our thoughts pertaining to God. As believers in Jesus, we have the authority to do what the Word of God says and "take captive every thought" (2 Cor. 10:5). We can quite literally pull down those destructive thoughts and replace them with a truth from God's Word. So, which will we choose? Will we allow what the Word of God says about us to shape our identities and determine our future, or will we listen to the voice and opinions of man?

There is a myriad of information bombarding us at every turn, which is why it is crucial that we know how to use Scripture as a weapon against the enemy's lies. Once we know God's perspective through His written Word, then we're free to align our belief systems and lives around that. This is where our identity as a child of God becomes rooted and grounded. I've noticed there has been a decline in true discipleship for new Christians over the last several years, and there are many people who do not have a solid understanding of how to read or fully understand the Bible. Can I take a moment to challenge you to dive into a solid Bible plan or Bible study, or a small group? It is a game changer, and I personally am so thankful for the believers I was surrounded by when I first came to faith many years ago. They opened my eyes to the reality that God gave us His written Word as our manual to follow in every area of life. I cannot grasp how you can be a true disciple of Christ but not understand your need to study and apply what the Word of God says. Maybe you find yourself picking and choosing the parts you like and want to follow, but that's not how it works. Jesus went to the cross and gave up His life for yours and mine, and became the living Word for each of us. When we follow the Word, we are following Jesus. Please hear me out: I'm not looking to ruffle any feathers here. But we live in a generation that lives for what feels good in the moment. God is full of grace, but He also gave us a guide that will help us make the right decisions. Do you need relationship help? It is in there. Help with your business? It is in there. Financial wisdom? It's there too. Thank You, God, for knowing we would need this and supplying a Book to help us navigate it all. If you don't know where to start, I would love to suggest opening the book of John and reading about the life of Jesus. Maybe start by simply reading a psalm or a proverb a day. There are so many incredible Bible studies available as well.

Have you ever thought about the fact that every answer we need can be found in Scripture? When we read the Word of God we get to know the heart of the Father and can then align our lives to reflect His teachings. Most of our beliefs about ourselves are formed as children. We learn from our parents (or whoever raised us), and the voices of those who are most influential in our lives shape our belief systems. Here is an example: if you grew up in a family with a mother or father who spoke things into your identity, such as "You are beautiful. You are special. God has a call on your life," then those positive affirmations would cause your adolescent brain and heart to believe that you are worthy and accepted. You would have a powerful sense of self-esteem and a deep-rooted belief that God has a great plan for your life even at an early age. However, what happens if we flip that narrative? Instead, what if you grew up hearing, "You're too fat. You're so draining. You won't ever amount to much"? Those are all negative and hurtful words that can also shape the way children begin to see themselves. Most of the issues, triggers, wounds, and struggles we carry into adulthood can be traced back to the childhood wounds we've never worked through. Here's the good news: there is always freedom and healing in Christ. At times it requires peeling back several layers of a wound when something happens in our lives that hits that sensitive spot. There is nothing better to tend to those sore places than the truth of God's Word. This is also where you can begin to be set free!

When we read the Word of God we get to know the heart of the Father and can then align our lives to reflect His teachings.

Let's look again at 2 Corinthians 10:5, where it says, "We demolish arguments and every pretension that sets itself up against the knowledge of God, and we take captive every thought to make it obedient to Christ." So, what does that look like in a practical sense? The primary point here is that we are in spiritual warfare. In verses 3–4 of the same chapter, Paul states that "though we live in the world, we do not wage war as the world does. The weapons we fight with are not the weapons of the world. On the contrary, they have divine power to demolish strongholds." This is why we must daily renew our minds with the Word of God. We can test and see what lines up with the truth of Scripture and not just live for what our flesh desires. Trusting God means we trust that His Word is the ultimate truth and instruction manual for life.

Now, back to the thoughts that we think! If we have not allowed the Lord to fully heal the broken and wounded places of our lives, we will be walking and talking with unhealthy thoughts and speech. This not only directly affects us, but eventually it will affect everyone around us as well. This is why it is so important we tend to our hearts. We do not have the luxury of stuffing things down or making our lives so full that we are simply coasting on autopilot until our next inevitable crash. Prayer is a beautiful place to start if you find yourself living in emotional survival mode. Take time to ask the Lord if there have been any word wounds in your past that are shaping the way you see yourself or what you believe about yourself, others, and especially, God. The Lord might bring to mind a certain person, conversation, or recurring thought you are being plagued with. You may sense an invitation from the Holy Spirit to forgive a specific person, or perhaps, yourself. There are many limiting beliefs and lies the enemy would like us to believe. The spirit of rejection and abandonment is so prevalent in our society and may be something you have walked through. Maybe you are wrestling with jealousy, insecurity, lying, or secretly feeling like everyone else is "winning" but you. We all battle various lies, but there is not a single area in our lives that His hand can't heal. You can take every wound to the Lord and allow Him to show you where the door was opened and the lies first crept in. You can ask Him what He would say about the situation and choose to replace negative thoughts with truth statements like "I am accepted in Christ. I belong to the Lord and the body of believers. I am free in Him." Insert whatever truth you need so you can see a breakthrough in that area.

I will often ask the Lord what He thinks about what I'm walking through. There was one instance where I sensed the gentle nudge of the Holy Spirit say, "If it broke your heart, then it broke Mine too." It brought me so much peace to know that God was with me and fighting for me. The Bible says, "'It is mine to avenge; I will repay,' says the Lord" (Rom. 12:19). We do not have to retaliate or get back at someone for being unkind because God will deal with them just as He is working on our hearts. Our posture should be to forgive, release, and bless ... then let God take care of the rest. That always brings me so much comfort. If you are in a season of life where you are striving to stay in the game or fight for your healing and breakthrough, can I challenge you to watch what you are thinking about and speaking out in that area? Just as we help our physical bodies by working out, walking, and eating well, we help our minds by putting the good stuff in and taking each thought captive.

What Are You Dwelling On?

Have you ever had a recurring thought that you just cannot seem to get out of your head? In counseling they can call this "rumination," which is a cycle of negative thinking. I always recall my early piano lesson days where we would loop scales back and forth to work on our hand technique. Over and over and up and down the keyboard. This repetition was building great hand-eye coordination. But for our thought patterns, we need to make sure we are building upon the right things, or we will be up and down all the time. According to the American Psychiatric Association, the negative aspect of rumination can contribute to the development of depression or anxiety, and can worsen existing conditions.[1] Wow. That's clearly not a pattern we want to find ourselves stuck in, even though we've all probably been there at some point along this journey.

I can remember a time where I really, really liked this guy. You know, the kind of situation where you read into everything even though it probably means nothing, and you think God is showing you signs left and right? Talk about being in la-la land. I'm sure you've been there too. Love is such a beautiful gift from God. Did you know He is the originator and author of love? God IS love. Everything about His character is wrapped up in that one character trait. It is the very center of the gospel and the good news of Jesus! "For God so loved the world that he gave his one and only Son, that whoever believes in him shall not perish but have everlasting life" (John 3:16). If we are not careful, though, we can allow our minds to twist and distort things, even when it comes to love. The situation I found myself in became worse when I finally realized this guy just wasn't into me. Looking back, I can see so many reasons why the Lord did not allow that relationship to flourish, but in the moment, my mind got fixated on thoughts that were way less than. I began to ruminate and believe lies that I was not smart enough, pretty enough, or skinny enough for this man. I began to loop conversations we had and things I had said out of a pure place and questioned whether he understood that. The enemy loves to bring chaos and confusion, and that is definitely what was happening in this situation. I finally had all I could take one day and took it to God in prayer. I had to come out of agreement with these thought patterns and see it for what it really was: a complete and total distraction from the purposes of God in my life in that season. Yes, we are all human and we all face disappointments that cause us to question ourselves, but this was becoming destructive. I had to choose to either believe what God says and thinks about me or constantly wonder what this guy was thinking and place my worth in his hands.

It took time and attention on my part to get my thought life back in order. Have you ever heard the term "vain imagination"? As someone who has a vast imagination, I have to keep it in line, so to speak. What is a vain imagination? Essentially, it is a furtive thought that lingers on your mind and begins to wear a rut, repeating itself constantly. It could be a false hope or an unfounded fear. Whatever it is, it doesn't belong in your head because it is not fruitful.

God has given us the authority over our minds to guard our thoughts and meditate on things above. It doesn't mean it will always be easy, but having the mind of Christ and walking in peace far outweighs anything the world has to offer. For some, words seem to roll off a little easier than for others. I always wanted to have tough skin, so to speak, but I've also realized being a bit more sensitive can be a superpower. You sense things, feel things, and see things that others may fail to. I have learned that people who tend to be the most critical about others are typically critical of themselves as well. Self-hatred sounds scary until you realize that if you operate out of a critical spirit, there just might be some underlying wounds that haven't been dealt with. You may not even recognize this is your own life. Take a tally of all the thoughts you have today. Begin with yourself, and then move on to others. You can list as many as possible and see if your thoughts build people up or tear them down. If this is something you struggle with, then you might want to consider if there are areas your heart has not experienced the full revelation of how much God has forgiven you and how much He loves you. Once we receive a revelation on this, it becomes easier to extend that same love, forgiveness, and grace to other people, especially the ones who are a bit more challenging to love.

God has given us the authority over our minds to guard our thoughts and meditate on things above.

If there is one message I could speak over you in this chapter, it is that your thoughts determine the course of your life. You can believe anything is possible with God, or you can believe nothing good is ever going to happen and watch that reality begin to take root. Our thoughts carry power, so much so that we can create new neural pathways with the right thoughts.

Something I have to continue to practice this side of my healing is speaking to my mind when my body starts acting in ways it did with Lyme disease. I still get triggered. I dealt with severe Covid where I thought I had the disease again because it mimicked many of the same symptoms. I had to tell myself daily, *"This is going to pass. It is not the same as 2019. You will get through this."* It's important that we look at the root of the thought. For me, it was rooted in fear that I would lose my health again and not be able to do the things I felt called to, all while being trapped in a body that was not functioning the way God intended it to. Here are a few statements to declare if you are battling a chronic illness:

> "God created my body to heal."
> "I am an overcomer."
> "By HIS stripes, I am healed."

Write them down, declare them out loud, and begin to believe it. I very rarely say, "I have this disease," or "I have a chronic illness." I want my mind and cells to hear this instead: "I am HEALING from Lyme, and I am overcoming chronic illness." To this day, there are still some repercussions and things from that awful disease that I deal with, but I try to put it in its proper place instead of allowing fearful thoughts to take me down a rabbit hole. Did you know your body's cells respond to your thoughts? This is why it's so important to make sure you are meditating on life-giving thoughts. Shame, guilt, and a victim mentality will affect various parts of our bodies and organs. There are so many scientific studies that prove the effects of these lower thought patterns and how they can eventually cause disease. If this is where you are today, there is no shame! I know long seasons of suffering have a way of breaking us down, but I also like to remember that we serve a God who is in the rebuilding business. He can bring beauty from ashes and joy from mourning. Here's the kicker, though: it's going to take intentionality to renew the mind daily.

John 10:10 says, "The thief comes only to steal and kill and destroy; I have come that they may have life, and have it to the full." One of the ways we experience that fullness of life is in our thought patterns. According to research, the average person has approximately sixty thousand thoughts per day. That is some serious thinking! Renewing our mind is vital, but something else I have found to be helpful is the power of visualization. Some might call it prophetic vision or speaking in accordance with God's Word. You might be thinking this is some kind of new age technique, but I promise it's not! Did you know we can partner with the Holy Spirit in all things? He is our comforter, teacher, and guide, and He leads us into all truth as we follow after Him. Now, let me be clear. I am not talking about envisioning a million dollars falling from the sky as you sit around all day and watch Netflix. That is a "name it and claim it" mentality. I am talking about asking God for direction in your current season and envisioning the things that He brings to your heart and mind. Let's take my season of overcoming health challenges, for example. I could partner my thoughts with what I was experiencing, which was lying around all day with very little energy, or I could begin to live out my faith and believe what God says is actually true.

Psalm 118:17 says, "I will not die but live, and will proclaim what the LORD has done." I began to speak this truth out, even when I didn't feel it, and would envision this in my life. I pictured myself playing tennis again, taking the long walks in nature that I always loved, flying all over the world, singing and ministering to people … the list goes on and on. Instead of partnering with the spirit of fear and death, I saw LIFE and life more abundant through Him.

This is a powerful tool to help overcome the schemes of the enemy. Is there an area where this might help you? I challenge you to set your alarm for five minutes and begin to visualize what you sense the Holy Spirit is declaring over your life. Is it regarding singleness? Well, begin to stand on the scripture that says, "It is not good for the man to be alone" (Gen. 2:18). Perhaps you can picture what your role would look like as a wife. How would you serve your husband? What would your new roles and schedules be like? I am not saying this is going to happen immediately, but I do believe it will increase your faith and vision. The Bible makes it clear that it is our faith that pleases the Lord, so no wonder that is where the enemy comes after us so often! It begins in our thoughts and words, so let's guard those and go on the offense. Fear is the opposite of faith, so if we are caught up in only seeing, speaking, and believing the worst will happen, that cannot please God. I recently took a poll on my social media accounts to see what lies and negative thought patterns plague people the most, and here were the resounding answers:

1. That I am not enough.
2. That I am forgotten by God.
3. That I am a failure.

We know these statements are not what the heart of the Father would speak over any son or daughter and are, in fact, the exact opposite of what God says. He reminds us of these truths:

1. You are never alone. I am WITH YOU ALWAYS (see Matt. 28:20).
2. I will never leave you nor forsake you. You are NOT ALONE (see Heb. 13:5).
3. Christ is the ONE who makes us righteous, not our own good works (see Phil. 3:9).

The enemy loves to twist things around in our minds because if he can get us to think about it and dwell on it, and build his case against us, then we will begin to believe it. So, let's be mindful of our initial thoughts and reactions. I have repeatedly seen in my own life, and in the lives of others, that the area where you have the greatest authority is typically where you will wrestle the most.

Take Out the Trash

What are the things that fight the hardest for our attention and thoughts? Social media is definitely the first thing that comes to mind. It is such a drain to our thoughts, not to mention a huge distraction from what's most important in our lives. It keeps us from spending time with the Lord and interacting with people in the way we were created to. You can easily wander down a rabbit trail of reels, links, articles, and pictures, and before you even know it, hours have gone by. It's very subtle, but we can quickly fall into unhealthy patterns of comparison and judgment, and then jealousy can creep in without warning. I have found it helpful to take social media breaks as they encourage you to evaluate your relationship to these apps. The first thing I noticed when I put my phone down was all the extra time I finally had on my hands to fulfill my calling. My creativity began to come back to life, and I felt energized in a way I never could when I was constantly bombarded with curated images on everyone else's highlight reels. I had a newfound clarity, my brain fog was lifted, and my heart felt so much lighter and freer. My relationships began to flourish and grow deeper because I was making a concerted effort to focus on the people in front of me and listen without distraction. Please hear my heart: I am not against Instagram or other social media platforms, but when it comes to our minds and our thought patterns, I do feel it can invite more clutter and distraction than abundant fruitfulness. Let's be more aware and do inventory on the place it holds in our lives.

Another area that's easy to get sucked into in our modern-day world is mindlessly binge-watching TV shows or movies. Also, what about listening to podcasts 24-7? All of these can cloud our minds and vision from the eternal things that matter most. For those of you who grew up in the '80s and '90s, do you remember how much time we spent playing outside? Or how much time we hung out with neighborhood children and were involved in extracurricular sports, music, dance, etc.? Things have drastically shifted, and now, instead of going out for a nice walk or to hang out with a friend, we will spend hours binge-watching our favorite shows. I am so guilty of this! I was asking the Lord about it one day, and I sensed that it has become a way for us to escape from the responsibilities of life, even for a moment. This world is full of so much overstimulation, and for many, it is simply a way to check out. I know having your lineup of favorite shows to watch or podcasts to listen to is not necessarily bad, but if they become an escape or something we do to numb the pain and pressure of life, then we need to take note. I know we all need time to withdraw and refill to keep our minds and thoughts fully optimized. If we look at the life of Jesus, He would often take time away and withdraw from the crowd. In a world defined by an often-untenable pace of performance and service, Scripture beckons us to an unhurried holiness, to withdraw with Jesus to desolate places. "Great crowds gathered to hear him and to be healed of their infirmities. But he would withdraw to desolate places and pray" (Luke 5:15–16 ESV). If Jesus needed time to regroup and pray, how much more do we need that solitude? We must follow His example, first and foremost. If we are going to remain standing in this world, then we must make sure we are filling our minds, spirits, and lives with heavenly things.

If we are going to remain standing in this world, then we must make sure we are filling our minds, spirits, and lives with heavenly things.

Let's take some time together to go over ways we can be replenished and refilled:

1. Studying Scripture to replace the lies with the truth.

2. Listening to solid teaching, preaching, and messages.

3. Being out in nature to renew your mind.

4. Moving and exercising.

5. Spending time with other believers. Healthy community is vital! Who you hang out with will either sharpen you and draw you closer to the Lord or draw you away.

6. Speaking the truth out loud. If you are really stuck in an area, write out verses and place them around your home, in your car, and on your mirrors. This will help your eyes, ears, and heart to catch up to the areas of your mind you need to renew.

Journal

Chapter 7

GRATEFUL THROUGH THE WAIT

If you're in an in-between season, the waiting can feel as though it is drowning you out. The tension between the deep desire for breakthrough to happen while feeling like you have been in transition forever can be exhausting. This is not the time to shrink back and simply coast, although that is tempting. No, this is the time to switch our perspective from what has not yet happened to all God has already done. We can choose to walk with an attitude of gratitude or an attitude of grumbling. There is a beautiful gift in this season to see, receive, and live out. I do not know many people who truly enjoy waiting. We live in a microwave generation and want everything in ten seconds or less. Like anything in life, we value things, and they mean so much more when we have to work hard or wait for them to come to pass.

Did you know that gratitude to God is a joyful emotion? When gratitude is turned toward God, we have a sense of joyful indebtedness for who He is and for His grace in our lives. In a sense, in the very emotion of gratitude, we are still the beneficiaries. Gratitude glorifies the Giver. When we feel thankful, we acknowledge our need and God's benevolence, God's fullness, and the very riches of His glory. People ask me all the time, "How are you so joyful even though some of the biggest prayers and desires of your heart have not come to pass yet?" I often smile and think, *If they only knew my whole story instead of just a few areas of the "not yet."* The key to living a joyful life in the in-between is being grateful for what you do have. As a Christ follower, if God never fulfilled one more desire or dream, I have already received everything I need in life: Him. Knowing I have been saved from death to life, knowing I will live eternally with Him, and knowing I belong to Him. Shouldn't that be enough for us all to be excited about this life here on earth and even more excited for the one to come? Have you had a revelation of how much God loves you? That will turn your striving into a position of being seated as a son or daughter and any impatience into a joy to wait on the Lord. We need to go back to the greatest gift we have or will ever be given ... the gift of salvation, which is life in Christ.

Gratitude glorifies the Giver.

Gratitude is a choice we make every day. It is a mindset and a posture of the heart. For some, living with gratitude comes easily, especially if you are naturally a positive person. Others will have to choose to be grateful and make it a daily practice. Just like spiritual disciplines, walking in gratitude can shift the entire course of your life. Did you know that when we are in a state of thankfulness, we can set a miracle in motion? On the contrary, if we are weighed down by anxious thoughts and constant dread, we set despair in motion. One of the many things I love about this life of faith is that God gives us choice. We are not walking robots. He allows us the opportunity to live in a place of surrender and gratitude, if we choose that. We will have seasons where it naturally flows out of us more than other times, but we must be aware of the condition of our soul. Just like building our physical muscles, we can build our gratitude muscles. In Psalm 9:1–2, we are instructed to give thanks: "I will give thanks to the LORD with my whole heart; I will recount all of your wonderful deeds. I will be glad and exult in you; I will sing praise to your name, O Most High" (ESV).

King David is one of the best examples of this, constantly choosing to praise God and put Him above his trials. He wrote most of the psalms in the Bible where we can see and feel his heart of gratitude. Even in the depth of the valley or while making poor decisions, it was his heart posture that gave him the title "a man after [God's] own heart" (Acts 13:22). Too often we look at the magnitude of our problem before we look at the magnitude of our God. It is a simple shift, but a powerful one.

So how do we choose gratitude? A great place to start is with the areas you are waiting on. Yes, I just said that. Thank God for the things that have not happened yet. Be grateful for the nos, the delays, and the timing that is not your own. Why? Because you are positioning your heart in a way that shows you ultimately trust Him no matter the outcome. At the root of gratitude is a deep trust in God's ways. If you know He is good, and you know all His ways are good, then you cannot help but be thankful. While we may not always feel grateful *for* everything that happens, I believe we can be grateful *in* everything, knowing that God is on the throne and we are not. You either trust He is in control, or you have some areas you are still holding tightly to.

Thank God for the things that have not happened yet. Be grateful for the nos, the delays, and the timing that is not your own.

I had a disappointment a few weeks ago while writing this book. I had worked hard for something in my music career and, for the first time in my life, felt that it might actually happen. I was wrestling in the weeks leading up to it. I wanted to believe it could happen, while also not wanting to put too much hope in it and be disappointed. I kept wrestling back and forth in a place of belief, faith, and gratitude, but I was also trying to protect my heart in case it didn't turn out the way I wanted. Finally, I just decided I was going to go all in and believe God for this. At that moment, something shifted as I chose gratitude for even being in a place and season of my life that this could potentially happen. Instead of believing for that one thing to come to pass, I realized the blessing was actually being in a place to have that kind of opportunity. I began to see the many miracles that had happened along the way to get me to this point. I began to see the answered prayers. I began to see just how good God had been to me from the smallest things to the biggest things, from the hardest of seasons to the best of them. I also realized the greatest gift was that I never gave up. There have been so many times in my musical journey when I just wanted to throw in the towel and be done. But God. He would gently tell me to keep going, not for man's applause but for Him alone. To not worry about success in the eyes of the industry but the ministry that was happening in His eyes.

I wish I could tell you that all my gratitude made that little dream come true, but it did not go the way I hoped. I got a big fat NO and, honestly, had my first real taste of what I'm sure is in every industry but I've been protected from for years. In that moment, I knew I had an invitation to be grateful for the rejection or to be totally taken out by the situation. It made little sense in some ways, but it was an opportunity to see if I really trusted God. Now, I'm not saying to be void of emotion. I grieved, was angry, felt sad ... all the things. I realized something through it all, though. I realized there are greater gifts if our eyes are open to see them.

As an independent artist, there can be tough roads along the way, and there are times you feel like you are doing it all on your own. What I came to realize was the amount of support, respect, and outpouring of love from my peers in the industry far outweighed the thing I was hoping for. There is usually an unseen gift or lesson in every trial if we are willing to dig deeper. It was also a needed reminder to put my hope not in the things of this world but, instead, in that which carries eternal significance. It took me a week and several conversations with trusted peers to navigate through it, but I slowly began to thank God it did *not* happen. I began to say things like "You see things that I do not" and "There is a reason that it wasn't supposed to work out." I began to thank God from a sincere place of gratitude that He knows what is best for me. The heaviness of it all began to lift, and a new determination to keep the focus on what God had done, and is doing, was reborn.

There is usually an unseen gift or lesson in every trial if we are willing to dig deeper.

Gratitude Keeps You Grounded

Gratitude will keep you grounded and moving forward in the darkest of days. I think it is one of God's greatest weapons for us to live this abundant life. Many people believe that abundance equals earthly things such as money, cars, homes, and other material items, but what does the Bible mean when it talks about living an abundant life? While He wants us to thrive in every area, including financially, I believe He is mostly referring to the fruit of the Spirit. To live a life of love, joy, peace, patience, long-suffering, perseverance, goodness, faithfulness, gentleness, and self-control (see Gal. 5:22–23). These fruits come from a posture of gratitude. This is where the real abundant living gets good ... when you can walk in these ways in and through every season. Our culture is addicted to stress, busyness, success, fame, huge bank accounts, statuses, and the list goes on. Oh, that we would see how futile and earthly all that is. There really is very little eternal significance in any of it. Don't get me wrong, the Lord desires for us to prosper in Him and to live an abundant life in Christ, but that has so much more to do with prospering in our souls. There is nothing wrong with earthly blessings, as long as they do not become idols.

Everything comes back to that heart position of surrender. When you are barely hanging on in life, and it takes everything you have just to take that next step, that is the perfect time to praise Him. We all have something we can be grateful for each day. If you woke up with breath in your lungs, then God is not done with you here on earth. If you woke up with two legs that move, thank God for the ability to go for a walk. There are many people bedridden or in wheelchairs who dream of a sunset stroll with two functioning legs. When we are in tough seasons, whether that be in our health, relationships, or finances, that is the time when we must pull ourselves out of self-pity and a victimhood mentality, and into a posture of thanksgiving. If we do not take this approach, then a bitter root of ungratefulness and disappointment will spring forth, causing our emotions, minds, bodies, and relationships to suffer. It starts subtly, so be alert.

We all have something we can be grateful for each day.

One of the ways we can grow in gratitude is by reframing our viewpoint. As believers, we need the help of the Holy Spirit to do this. Did you know that when you came to salvation, God placed His Spirit within you to guide and lead you into all truth? So what does that look like, practically speaking? I'm going to use an example from my healing journey to help you navigate living a more abundant life filled with gratitude.

When I was unable to physically do much of anything, I remember how long the days felt. I missed social interactions, daily movement, and dreaming into the future. There were days where I felt completely stuck in a body that would not do what I knew God created it to do. I tried everything in the Spirit to stay hopeful, but it took something more specific to see a real shift. I began to thank God for the season I was in, not the one I was *hoping* for. I began to thank God that He was causing a forced pause and major slowdown in my life. Now, I know you may be asking yourselves, "But God is not the author of sickness, is He?" I couldn't agree more; however, we live in a fallen world where sickness abounds. I had no idea why I got bit by a tick that would eventually wreak havoc in my life. What I do know is that God is sovereign over all things. I clung to a scripture during this time that was very personal to me, since my birthday is 8/28. Romans 8:28 says, "And we know that all things work together for good to those who love God, to those who are the called according to His purpose" (NKJV). What I did not realize is that this passage is arguably the most sought-after verse in the Bible for comfort in times of distress.

I would also make a list and repeat several of the good things in my life that were included on that list. The first was the gift of being with my family. I had moved out when I was seventeen years old, and then to Seattle, and later to Nashville. I had not been back home in over twenty years, other than for holidays and occasional birthdays. It was incredibly humbling to be back in my parents' house at the age of forty-three, barely able to function. But it turned out to be the most unexpected gift.

Another way I began to reframe this forced slowdown was to remind my soul of the ways the Lord had provided abundantly in prior seasons. I was able to take off from work without struggling financially. That was a gift I would not take for granted as there had been past seasons of drought. During that time, I would listen to old demos on my phone since it was too painful to read, sing, or play piano with a 24-7 neurological Lyme headache from the pit of hell. As I lay there listening, something began to take place that had never happened before. The words and lyrics to some of the demo songs I had worked on prior to getting sick began to minister to my own soul. One of these songs, titled "All Things," is actually about God working all things for our good. God reframed that season where these songs were speaking to me even if no one ever heard them. My own spirit was responding to them, which was truly a gift.

If you feel stuck in a particular area or feel bitterness beginning to creep in, will you take a moment to invite the Holy Spirit to show you the gifts of the place you find yourself in? Begin to reframe your situation to find the good despite the not-so-good circumstances happening around you. Just as we choose our words, thoughts, and joy, we can also choose gratitude in all things.

Grateful for the "Nos" and "Not Yets"

How many times in our lives do we thank God for the "nos" and "not yets"? When I was a new believer, I felt like every prayer I ever prayed came to pass, and quickly! Some might call that the honeymoon phase, similar to a marriage relationship, when everything feels a bit too perfect in the beginning. I can remember thinking, *Wow, I can just ask God for something, and it will come to pass!?* But I now realize because my faith muscles were small, God knew I needed to grow in my belief system and understanding of who He is, and trust

His nature and character. It is easy to ask God for something when your foundation is rooted and grounded in who He is. It is easy to be grateful when you know that the heart of Father God is always for you. When I was a young believer, He knew I was going to need a track record with Him for when bigger trials and tests came down the road. If you think about a good earthly father, he is not going to give his child every little thing they want every time they ask. That would be irresponsible. I mean, for those of us with a sweet tooth, that would be candy and desserts galore, which is not in our best interest. Our dads would be thinking of the cavities, prediabetes, weight issues, or worse that could potentially happen as a result. A young child cannot comprehend those things. There are safety and protection when God withholds something from us. There are things we might want but God knows it is not for our greater good in this season or place that we are currently in.

When God says no or not yet, it is not because He is holding out but because He is holding on to a greater gift at the right time. So, how do you stay in a place of gratitude when you might be hearing no after no after no? These are the times to strip things back and really work on our core foundations of faith. This might sound too simple, but what do you know to be true? I know that God does not withhold. Psalm 84:11 assures us "no good thing does he withhold from those whose walk is blameless." If my faith and confidence are in this truth, then I can be grateful that things didn't work out the way I hoped. I can look back to countless testimonies I have where I saw the tangible faithfulness of my Father. There are so many reasons to choose this posture of gratitude, but I feel one of the most prevalent reasons we need to hone this skill more than ever is because in a world that is trying to shut God out of everything, gratitude helps us see God in everything.

When God says no or not yet, it is not because He is holding out but because He is holding on to a greater gift at the right time.

It opens our spiritual eyes. There's a beautiful cycle in giving God thanks. The more we cultivate this and begin to thank Him, the more we will see Him working in us and around us. It helps us sense God's presence, His personal care, and His perfect timing!

Walking in gratitude also puts us squarely in His will. I don't know about you, but there are times where I overthink and make God's will out to be this mystical plan that I might somehow miss, when more times than not, it is simple obedience. We know His will for us is to be thankful, not just on the days where everything is going well but on the really challenging ones. So, the next time that "thing" doesn't work out in your favor or the door slams shut, can you begin to thank God even there? This will open your spiritual eyes to see God's hand over every circumstance. If you are battling with anxiety and fearful thoughts, can I suggest that it could be time to shift your gaze to every good thing that is happening in your life right now instead of focusing on what you desperately want to change?

Gratitude While Learning Grit

It was mid-March of 2020 when I got the call so many of us did during that time. I was on the Aspire women's event tour leading worship and sharing my story of overcoming. I had been off the road while I was healing from Lyme and had not toured like this in a while. I was nervous yet excited to share with women all over the country the hope we have in Christ. The question *Is my body going to be able to get through this grueling schedule post-Lyme?* flooded my mind. We had done two back-to-back weekends on the West Coast that went incredible, and I could feel my stamina coming back. I felt smack dab in the center of God's will again. When I returned to Nashville thinking I had a few days to do laundry, pack, and regroup before heading back out on the road, the promoter of the tour called. He told me that due to the world shutting down with this sickness called Covid we would most likely need to take the next few weeks off. That was such a bummer to hear for many reasons. It was my first tour after being sick and finally feeling good again, it is my job (which equals income), and none of us were prepared for what was coming next. That few weeks off turned into an entire spring and fall tour being canceled. I can remember in that moment sensing the Holy Spirit say, "You have two choices: you can be grateful I am in control, or you can start to grumble and complain." This began a journey of learning both gratitude and grit.

In a world that is trying to shut God out of everything, gratitude helps us to see God in everything.

God began to give me ideas of how I could still minister to people. I started *Worship Out Corona* on my Instagram live stories. I was overcome with the amount of people who were hungry for community through an app and wanted to worship and pray for healing for those who were affected by this awful illness. I learned new ways of generating income from online merch sales and promotions. I began to truly rest during that time, which may not sound like it took grit, but it required mental effort to slow down during what should have been my busiest season.

During this time, a sweet friend had gifted me with a gorgeous glass jar that had the word GRATEFUL in big gold letters. It came with little cards and a pen. The idea was to write down one thing you are grateful for each day and put it in the jar. In the midst of a pandemic, that forced me to find the good in things. When I look back on that season, I now realize that my health began to flourish again. There was ample time to write new songs, an album was born, and some beautiful breakthroughs took place. I often wonder if I had started to complain, grumble, or see only the negative, would all of that have still happened?

As I close this chapter, I want to leave you with a few questions to reflect on:

1. Are you only grateful when everything is going your way?
2. Have you made it a practice to choose gratitude and cultivate it in your daily life?
3. Would you consider grabbing your own version of a grateful jar or maybe begin to journal and write down the ways you see the Lord moving in your life?
4. Are there any bitter roots toward God, yourself, or someone else that could be blocking a life of thanksgiving?

I recently decided to dump all those little cards out of the jar. With tears streaming down my face, I was not only reminded of all that I am thankful for, but I saw many prayers come to pass through being grateful for things that had not yet happened but am now walking in. I remember thanking God in advance for what made no sense at the time. There is something powerful that takes place when we combine our faith with a grateful heart. It is a major key that will ground you, keep you humble, and help you remain in awe of God.

This is so much more than another motivational or self-help tool. This is a biblical principle that will yield good, good fruit in your life. I dare you to choose gratitude in *all* things.

Journal

Chapter 8

WHEN GOD WANTS YOU TO GROW

Ever feel like everything is just off? You can't seem to find your groove or firm step in life no matter how hard you try. These are usually signs that God is causing you to grow, and this happens the most while in the in-between and waiting seasons in life. God's greatest desire in our lives is that we would grow in character, godliness, and integrity and live this life of faith in real time. It's easy to get comfortable when everything *seems* to be going well or exactly as planned ... until something happens that knocks you off track.

In my journey with God, I have learned this happens one of two ways. The first is you begin to get uncomfortable. You know that God is shaking things up in your life to bring you to the next chapter, but it can be painful. The things that used to work no longer work. You are more aware of your need for Jesus and how easy it is to walk in the flesh instead of leaning into the Spirit and what God desires. When the pruning begins, it is an indication that God is growing and stretching you. This may look like God removing things such as people, friendships, or relationships that are not for your higher good or His purpose. Maybe you have a sudden job change or even an unexpected trial that hits. He might highlight where an area has become an idol in your life, even good, well-meaning things like career, goals, and dreams.

Don't be alarmed by the cutting away. He could be trying to get your attention or, quite possibly, causing you to slow down. There are circumstances that might not turn out how you wanted because He needs more of your heart surrendered to what He wants. Growth requires us to take a hard look at what is working and what is not. What is God highlighting in your life right now? If He is asking you to let go of something, make sure you yield to that. Obedience will yield the greatest fruit in our lives, but we must be willing to walk through uncomfortable and hard places. When a trial hits your life it's easy to think that the enemy is messing with you, but let's look at it from a different point of view. There are most definitely times in all our lives where the enemy tries to shake us and rattle us. A seasoned believer will see this for what it is: an attack from the evil one to distract, condemn, or bring confusion or shame, and ultimately, throw us off our God-given course. This is not the time to shrink back but to press in even more to who you know God to be. This is why I cannot stress enough how crucial it is for believers to know the

Word of God. So many people think they are wrestling with other people, flesh and blood, but the Scriptures make it clear that there is a spiritual realm, and we wrestle against principalities and spiritual forces. There is a spirit behind everything and in everyone. Make sure you are taking advice from people who are led by the Spirit and are displaying fruit in their daily lives.

Growth requires us to take a hard look at what is working and what is not.

Was there ever a time in your life where you could sense the attacks or, as the Word says, "the little foxes" that are trying every which way they can? Song of Songs 2:15 says, "Catch for us the foxes, the little foxes that ruin the vineyards, our vineyards that are in bloom." Pay attention to what is happening in your life during these seasons. Here are some of my notes from an online Bible study I did once that might help you if you are in that place:

> The "little foxes that ruin the vineyards," that hinder the growth and take away the tender fruit, are the sins of the spirit. This time the word "spirit" is spelled with a small "s." The "sins of the flesh" are the gross sins of adultery, murder, blasphemy,

> drunkenness, etc. The "sins of the spirit" are "the little foxes" that creep in almost unnoticed and spoil the vines and take away the fruit. What are these "little foxes," these "sins of the spirit"? There are three kinds: there are the wrong things we think, the wrong things we say, and the wrong things we do. These may be described as heart sins, lip sins and behavior sins.[1]

Below is also taken from the same online Bible study. I found this incredibly helpful in discerning what you are walking through when you feel like the attacks are happening on every side.

> *Think of the heart sins, the secret sins.* David had something to say about these in Psalm 51:10. What are they? They are sins such as jealousy, pride and impurity. These are "the little foxes that spoil the vineyards," the sins of the spirit that hinder the fruit of the Spirit in our lives. God can see these "secret" sins—look up Psalm 90:8.
>
> *There are the lip sins.* Do you ever pray the prayer recorded in Psalm 141:3? Or did you ever notice the testimony of the psalmist in Psalm 120:1–3? What a lot of harm this "little fox" of an unruly, undisciplined tongue can do, especially when it is

a lying tongue, a critical tongue or a tale-bearing tongue!

There are the behavior sins. These are sins that we commit when we act in such a way that it is obvious to an onlooker that we have an unclean heart and a wrong spirit—when we are unkind, thoughtless or harsh in our treatment of others, or when we are wrong in our relationship with another person.

The way to deal with "the little foxes" is to kill them. They must be rounded up and put to death (Galatians 5:24); they must be mortified (Romans 6:11). If the little foxes are not put to death they will grow into big foxes! For an illustration of the way to kill the little foxes read Judges 15:4–5 and turn to Romans 13:14. But how can we do this? We cannot do it in our own strength.

The way to kill "the little foxes" is to rely upon the Holy Spirit. We learn this from Galatians 5:16—"Live by the Spirit, and you will not gratify the desires of the sinful nature." Yield to the Holy Spirit, trust Him and rely upon Him to give you the victory. Then there will appear in your life an abundance of fruit—"the fruit of the Spirit."

I hope those scriptures are helpful for you to study if you sense you are under a spiritual attack. Take note of what is happening in your life during these seasons. I have come to learn that the strongest attacks typically come before one of my biggest breakthroughs or a ministry impact.

I am sure you have heard the old saying "new levels, new devils." I think there is some truth in this, so what can we do during these times to be more proactive? Besides making sure we are in the Word of God and studying Scripture (which is literal manna from God), it's also important to be in fellowship with other believers. There is an overwhelming amount of church hurt in our world right now. I am so sorry if you were wounded by a church, a leader, a pastor, or another believer. But can I gently remind you of something? No one is perfect except Jesus, including you. If you are holding back because of past church wounds, I would encourage you to do inner healing work. Forgive and get to the root of what is really holding you back. Is it childhood wounds and trauma you haven't dealt with that are affecting your filter, the way you view people, and your friendships and relationships? The enemy's number one goal is to keep you out of fellowship or community with other believers through the local church because he knows that we are stronger together. Isolation is one of the enemy's greatest tactics. Community brings life, accountability, and growth as well as helps us see where our own blind spots are, because we have trusted people in our lives who are committed to seeing us grow in our walks with God. This is not a time to shrink back in fear or ego, thinking we are better off on our own but to find a great local church that teaches the entirety of the Word. There are gifts within each one of us that people need, whatever community the Lord places you in. The more isolated we stay in our walk with God, the more offenses we end up picking up toward people.

I am not making light of very real wounds you may have, but it deeply saddens me when I see people stuck and disconnected instead of realizing there are great people and churches that can help in the healing journey, not hinder it. Here is a key if you are walking through this: A wounded heart = Suspicion. A healthy heart = Discernment. The health of your heart determines how accurately you will see. If we harbor bitterness, offense, or jealousy, or refuse to tend to heart wounds, then those will be the filters we see through while judging situations and other people. The more we allow God to heal and free us, the more accurately we can discern. And discernment is key for when God wants us to grow. We must be able to see things for what they are. I wish I could say being a believer means everything is easy breezy because we walk by faith, but that is simply not true. I think being a Spirit-led believer who is doing his or her best to partner with God in advancing the kingdom will put a target on your back. The enemy knows that if he can shut us down, then we will not be as effective. So, see it as you might be on track if you feel like all hell is literally breaking loose in your life.

A wounded heart = Suspicion. A healthy heart = Discernment.

In earlier chapters, we talked about how important it is to guard our thoughts and what comes out of our mouths. During a season of transition, growth, or in-between, it is so important to hone those skills. In order to step forward in growth, we have to be willing to assess where we are. Are we stuck? You can sense the pull of the Spirit drawing you into a new season, but the old is familiar and comfortable. Or are we being complacent? Is it easier just to keep things as they are instead of pressing into the new? Or perhaps fear has crippled you to a point where you cannot take that next step. The beautiful thing about this life of faith is how kind God is. I truly have seen time and time again that He does not make things hard, but there are times when we do. Can I get a witness to that!? Take a minute to take a deep breath and really assess where you are. Are you hearing from God in a place of healthy discernment? Do you have the courage and community around you for when He calls you to take that next step? Growth requires grace toward ourselves and others. I do not know many people who like change or enjoy rocking the boat, so to speak. The other day, I realized that many things I do professionally have become second nature because I have been doing them for over twenty years. Then God orchestrated this season of writing a book, and I had a wide array of emotions. I was so excited ... and then completely freaked out! This was out of my comfort zone and skill set (give me a piano and microphone any day!), but I knew God was asking me to do something new. I needed faith to write this book. I needed courage to truly lean into and trust God to help me.

A second way we might recognize God is stretching us is if He starts to speak the same message over and over directly through His Word or other people. If you feel like God is consistently speaking to you about a particular area, it's likely that He is trying to guide you in that direction. Maybe you hear a sermon by your pastor on Sunday morning and you think, *Wow, I just read that scripture yesterday!* Then, you're at lunch with a friend and she brings up the same thought, scripture, or challenge to you. My friend, this is a clear sign that God is trying to get your attention and speak to you. These are times we must press into that still, small voice and ask God to confirm what it is He is saying specifically through that verse and how He is using that to guide our next step. The fact that you picked up this book makes me think that God has been speaking to you about topics of surrender and waiting, and how to live in the in-between spaces as you wait on specific promises to come to pass. The Holy Spirit is always talking to us and leading us into His truth, but sometimes we must ask ourselves if we are really listening. God speaks most often through His written Word, so when we find ourselves being stretched in our faith or feeling a new season approach, we can ask God to confirm what we're sensing through His Word.

The Holy Spirit is always talking to us and leading us into His truth, but sometimes we must ask ourselves if we are really listening.

Another sign that God might be growing you is that new and unexpected doors are opening that you know you are not able to walk through on your own. I believe God does this because He knows that in order for us to really grow, something in our lives needs to shift. An unexpected opportunity, new relationship, or location change comes into our lives causing us to really see where our faith muscles are. If we have stayed grounded in His Word, prayer, and good community, these are times to move forward in faith with that support system already in place instead of shrinking back.

Is God asking you to shake things up? Maybe for some of you, this is simply coming back to Him and making your relationship with Jesus right. Maybe for others, you know God has been speaking to you for years to step out, but you have become complacent and comfortable in the place you are. Can I encourage you to take that next step and do whatever He is asking of you, not just for your own benefit but because God wants to bless people through you and your obedience. Or maybe you are like me, and you took that huge leap of faith and are currently trying to grow in the deep end. Congratulations! What a beautiful place to be because you will need to cling to Jesus and hold on to Him with all you have got. Isn't that this life of faith we are called to, though? Total and complete dependence upon God? I know too well the temptation when we are in a season of waiting or in-between to want to coast and just get by. There have been several seasons where I felt like I lost my good fight of faith, but you know what else I learned? The hardest seasons in my life have been where I felt the nearness of God the most and was walking dead center in the purpose He placed on my life. It is when I took crazy, scary steps of faith into the unknown and where my utter dependence on Him was strengthened. I will say it until I am blue in the face, but God is so much more concerned with who we are becoming in these seasons than with our comfortability. The reality is that, at any moment, God can shift you from waiting on it to walking in it. So, why not let all the growth, healing, purpose, and faith grow until that time comes?

God's Waiting Room

I don't know about you, but I have learned that I have one of those big ole hearts that can get hurt easily and never wants to hurt anyone else. Sadly though, we live in a broken world where people are going to break our hearts, and even when we try to live with the best intentions and motives, we will somehow hurt people's hearts as well. Goodness, that makes me long for heaven even more. Don't be surprised when God begins to prune your relationships while in the waiting rooms. If bad company corrupts good character, imagine what good company can do. There is a quote that I love by author and pastor Craig Groeschel. "Show me your friends, and I'll show you your future. The people you are hanging out with today are shaping the person you will become tomorrow."[2] God sees what we cannot. He knows where He is taking us, and He knows who will stay in it with us through every season.

If bad company corrupts good character, imagine what good company can do.

I choose to live in a place where I believe the best about people and their motives. Call me a bit naive (which is something I could work on!), but what you see is what you get. I have had to learn along the way that people are meant to be in your life for a season, are there to teach you a lesson, or are there for the long haul. Having a good community takes time, effort, a soft heart, and being willing to be a good friend through the good and bad. If you are a believer, it is so important to find those sisters and brothers in your life whom you can run hard after God with. People who really know you and will challenge you to be the best version of yourself. I sat in a room a few weeks ago with about twenty of my closest friends and realized how strategic it was of God to place these people in my life. Some I have known over thirty years … others only twenty, ten, or less than a year. As I was looking around that room at this birthday party feeling celebrated and loved on, I also realized the depth of trials, the journeys, and the highs and lows I have walked with many of them in my own life and in their lives. The prayers prayed for one another in different seasons, the celebrations and losses. When you are in the waiting room with God, it is important to have people around you who will worship, weep, and walk with you through it all. We learn the beauty of vulnerability with God and trusted friends.

One of the biggest lessons learned in the waiting rooms of God is how to persevere well. *Waiting* is an action word, and in the Hebrew it is *qavah*, meaning "binding together, eagerly waiting, hoping for, expecting."[3] This definition captures a sense of optimism and hope. We can be proactive as we wait for promises to be fulfilled. One of the ways we do this is by digging into the relationships that

God has put in our lives. Calling out the gold in others and allowing their comfort, challenge, and support to help us walk through the seasons we are in. One of the biggest keys to thriving in God's waiting room is to not put off living your life when you think you have all the missing puzzle pieces together. Start living that beautiful and vibrant life now. I know what you are thinking ... *But I want to get out of the waiting room and into the waters of fulfillment.* My challenge for you is: What if you can learn to be fulfilled even while you are waiting? You never wait alone. You wait with and on God, which can become one of the greatest adventures of your life. While you wait, God works.

While you wait, God works.

Waiting is a sustained effort to stay focused on God through prayer and belief. To wait is to "rest in the LORD and wait patiently for Him" (Ps. 37:7 NASB). Another thing that is most likely to take place as you are actively being prepared in the waiting room is the pruning. This is not always fun or easy but is necessary if we are going to fulfill everything God has placed on our lives and be able to carry the weight of it without being crushed by our own sin and pride. So, what does God's pruning process look like? John 15:1–2 says, "I am the true grapevine, and my Father is the gardener. He cuts off every branch of mine that doesn't produce fruit, and he prunes the branches that do bear fruit so they will produce even more" (NLT). This scripture is spoken by Jesus. In His own words He describes Himself as the Vine and us as the branches. The healthy branches will yield much fruit, whereas the useless ones will be gathered for the fire. In the original Greek, the word for "prune" in John 15:2 means "to cleanse." The only way to stay healthy is to remain in Him and stay connected to the Vine. Does the pruning sometimes hurt? Honestly, yes.

If God is going to cleanse something from you, then it means it is no longer in alignment with His will for you. This might include Him removing people or things that you feel are precious to you for His higher plans. We have to remember that He sees the bigger picture and knows exactly what we need even when it does not feel right or fair at times. We can either relax in that truth, fully trusting God's ways, or we can force something to happen. We can strive and try to make it work in our way and time. Why try to force the fruit though? The longer you try to extract the fruit from something that is sick or dead, the more you prolong the inevitable. By allowing things to be pruned off, you are letting yourself be cleansed, which will lead to greater peace, clarity, and purpose.

The joy that is ahead is worth any amount of pruning or cutting back. If you think about a fruit tree that has been pruned, it might take another season of growth for that to fully come into harvest. It is the same with us. We will walk through some cutting-away seasons as we sit patiently in the waiting room, but please remember as you yield to and obey God, the next season is coming. There will be a harvest in your life of growth, and new lush fruit will appear again. I am living proof that God gives and He takes away, but as you posture your heart to bless Him no matter what, you will find yourself living a full life even if some chapters have not yet come to fruition. Start living now, friend ... *really* living. Don't wait for that next job, breakthrough, career change, or relationship to happen. Plug yourself into the Vine—Jesus Christ—like never before and plug yourself into a great church and community. Allow yourself to bloom right where you are planted and then watch what God does. A new sense of purpose and joy will fill your life that has nothing to do with your outward circumstances. This is where the real living begins. I often say the act of learning to surrender all to God is truly an art. It is not necessarily something that comes easily to our flesh. It is much more normal for us to want to control things or do it our way.

There is nothing wrong with making plans, but if you tend to be someone who cannot go with the flow, then you might be holding too tightly to your plans instead of God's plan. A spirit of control can mask itself in many ways. Think about this for a moment ... Are you rattled when your plans change? Do you need to always be in control of a situation, or can you wait to see how circumstances play out? Do you react negatively when something doesn't go your way? If you answered yes to any of these, then I would encourage you to ask the Lord to give you the strength to release some control and truly live in a posture of surrender. Ask Him how to be led by His Spirit in a way where, no matter what, you trust Him. You trust Him when things work out the way you had hoped, and you trust Him when your plans come crumbling to the ground. You trust Him when the timetable looks completely backward to you by learning how to lean in and yield to the promptings of the Spirit. This will not happen overnight. It takes practice, a broken and contrite heart, and most of all, a heart yielded to Jesus.

We have covered a lot in this chapter! Let's take a moment to reflect and apply it all. When you have some quiet time, will you dig into the questions below? You can write them out or journal them. Ask the Holy Spirit to illuminate anything He wants to share with you as you read through these activation questions:

1. Is God shaking things up in your life? Have you grown comfortable or complacent as you wait for your season to shift? Pray into this and write down anything that comes to mind. Repent, if needed, and ask God for His action plan.

2. What "little foxes" are trying to get in to distract you and keep you from your fullest potential? Write these out and give them over to the Lord.

3. Are you resting and actively preparing in God's waiting room, or are you striving to quickly get to the next season?

4. Are you staying connected to the Vine? Are there areas that God is trying to cut back so that a greater harvest in your life can take place?

5. Is there an area you need to learn how to release control to God? Are you being Spirit-led or led by the desires of your flesh?

Journal

Chapter 9

MORE LOVE, LESS FEAR

Fear is very real in this generation. So many people talk about struggling with anxiety and worry in the times we live in. It has almost become the norm. The World Health Organization states that one in four adults struggled with some type of anxiety disorder in 2024.[1]

I think we have all been there. You get a pit in the bottom of your stomach; your mind starts to race, and the heart palpitations do not seem to want to slow down. I definitely have had a season or two where I felt more anxious than I ever have in my life. I began to investigate and dig a little bit deeper into what was causing this, in my own life and so many other people's lives. To my surprise, at the root of this epidemic of anxiety is the underlying emotion of fear. God must have known this was going to be an issue as the phrase "fear not" appears in the Bible 365 times, once for each day of the year. Some scholars believe that the phrase's frequent repetition in the Hebrew Bible makes it a common expression of reassurance.

Before I go any further on this topic, I want to be clear that I am not making light of any anxiety disorders, or if you are on medication, I am in no way trying to place shame or condemnation on a very real issue. Please hear my heart on this. You are free to be led to deal with this in the way God is leading you. My only goal is to bring a little more hope, light, and encouragement for those who are battling through this. God desires freedom in every area of our lives, and I know firsthand that, through the power of the Holy Spirit, we can overcome any mental torment.

God runs on love, but a very real enemy of our soul, Satan, runs on fear. Some of the biggest hurdles to overcome while in seasons of waiting or the in-between are anxiety and depression. Guess what? Both of these are rooted in fear. The more uncertain a season feels, the more we begin to wonder where God is. I believe this is one of the biggest setups from the enemy. If he can cause us to doubt that God is engaged in our lives or that He really cares for us, then a spirit of fear will begin to manifest in our lives. As mentioned in earlier chapters, this fear can also creep in during seasons of deep discouragement and sadness. At the root of it all is questioning where God is in our greatest time of need. Time and time again we are commanded in the Bible to "fear not." So, what does God *really* say about fear? The answer is pretty simple:

do not be afraid. We can rest in the words of Isaiah 41:10, which say, "Fear not, for I am with you; be not dismayed, for I am your God; I will strengthen you, I will help you, I will uphold you with my righteous right hand" (ESV).

God runs on love, but a very real enemy of our soul, Satan, runs on fear. Some of the biggest hurdles to overcome while in seasons of waiting or the in-between are anxiety and depression.

I know it's easy to say "do not fear" and to read these scriptures, but how do we walk this out on a day-to-day, practical basis? I think the best place to start is by learning more about the opposite of what fear is: love. Did you know love is the greatest force on earth because God is love? It is the very essence of His being, so everything He does is rooted in love.

One of the most cherished and googled scriptures in the Bible, and one I know so many believers cling to, is 1 John 4:18: "There is no fear in love. But perfect love drives out fear, because fear has to do with punishment. The one who fears is not made perfect in love." Have you ever noticed the way you feel physically or emotionally when you are in love? It kind of feels like you are walking on clouds, the birds are singing louder, and the skies look a little bluer.

You might have an extra spring in your step and more energy than normal. This is because every cell of your body and mind is being flooded by the greatest life force God ever created. Everything in life should stem from God's love and then flow through people, family, friends, and significant others. Truly, love has the power to heal. It heals hearts, bodies, minds, and souls, and the author of this love is God Himself.

As believers, the reality is we do not have to be afraid of anything when we are the beloved of God. We can be confident that we belong to Him in the family of God. We have been fully forgiven of sins, which means we should not feel shame in any way, even in our shortcomings. God will lead us by His conviction, which leads us to hope. Either Christ is enough to forgive, heal, and set free, or we are doing things in our own strength to try to gain acceptance and worth. The one who knows and lives for Christ is in true fellowship and does not need to fear future punishment. The person who experiences constant fear has not experienced perfect love. In other words, those who fear punishment do not have a complete or mature relationship with God.

This was hard for me to grasp for a while. I thought I had experienced the love of God, and in many ways I had. But there were still cracks in my foundation that the Lord was trying to heal. Until we take our last breath here on earth, we will be growing and evolving in the love and knowledge of God. We will never arrive, but we can continue to grow closer and closer to Him. A heart that has been fully enveloped in the perfect love of Jesus will fear nothing. That means that bad reports, slander, the unknown, or anything else will not cause them fear because their foundation is rooted in the unconditional love of God. For many of us, though, we fear we will be punished in some way or that something bad is going to happen to us because we have not been a perfect Christ follower. This mindset is such a trap and scheme of the enemy. Let's expose it for what it is ... A LIE. This is a way the enemy tempts us to be self-focused and live in shame and regret instead of walking confidently in our identity as a son or daughter of the Most High.

A heart that has been fully enveloped in the perfect love of Jesus will fear nothing.

So, how do we receive more of the love of God? We allow His perfect love to literally cast out the fear and turmoil in our hearts. This is a daily practice and one that will yield so much good fruit in our lives. This is an area that I have personally felt called to press into and overcome. I remember how strongly a spirit of fear wanted to enter in on the day I first learned about Lyme disease. I made the mistake of researching it and somehow ended up on late-stage Lyme. It was devastating to read. Word to the wise: just skip googling any medical symptoms. It rarely helps and is too tempting to go down rabbit holes that lead to worst-case scenarios. I had all the symptoms, so it threw my mind and heart into a downward spiral. Looking back on this time, I wish I had immediately taken those fearful thoughts and placed them into the hands of Jesus. You see, I trusted God as my healer and my faith was strong, so I believed I was going to get through it and overcome, but I allowed fear to play with my mind for far too long.

We can open the door to things in our lives that oftentimes we are not even aware of. What thoughts and beliefs are we partnering with that are causing a root of fear to develop? If my heart is fearful in any way, then that just means there is an area where I have not allowed the love of God to perfect. Once I was aware of how the enemy was using this fear tactic in my life, I began to go on the offense. I began to declare the love of God out loud and visualize it filling every crevice and crack in my foundation. Sometimes you have to come out of agreement with things, so I began to confess, repent, and declare that I would not be ruled by fearful thoughts and the what-ifs of that diagnosis. I began to believe and live in a posture where the peace, words, and love of God would be the things I would stand upon. It took time and practice, but every instance where I would feel that grip on my heart, I would close my eyes and say, *"God, may Your perfect love flow straight to that place that is afraid."* The more you do something, the more it becomes a habit and then a lifestyle. Before I knew it, my heart posture was more and more secure in love and less open to fear. You also might have to allow the Holy Spirit to do inner-healing heart work, as we have discussed in earlier chapters. Ask the Lord to show you the first time you really experienced a spirit of fear. There may be something that comes to your memory that you are already aware of, or it might be something in your subconscious. We all have generational patterns and sins that have been passed down from our family line. Maybe you have learned that your grandmother was anxious, your mom was anxious, and now you are anxious. This is a pattern that can be broken in Jesus' name! You can be the one in your family line to break free and set up the generations to come in wholeness in this area.

Once you have received some insight on where this might have started, it's as easy as taking it to the Lord and asking Him to deliver you from it. This works in any area of our lives, not just with fear. Ask Him to show you where He was in that memory and moment, and how His sacrifice for you is more than enough to set you free.

Over the last several years, I have had the great honor of being part of a prayer team called Liberty, where we walk people through inner healing sessions. It is a bit like counseling, but all led by the Holy Spirit directing hearts into freedom. This area of fear was always one that would come up.

In one of the sessions, we were bringing a young gal through some healing around family molestation that she had dealt with as a child. She had gone through intensive Christian counseling and was in such a better place but kept sensing the Lord was digging deeper into her heart. She wanted to break this pattern off of her family's lives as she knew she was not the first to encounter this. So, we started there. There are many great prayers to pray into this, and if you are curious and want to dig even deeper, a great resource is *Freedom Tools: For Overcoming Life's Tough Problems* by Andy Reese and Jennifer Barnett. We then moved on to that first moment she remembered being overwhelmed and paralyzed by a spirit of fear. She shared with us details of the night. There were people she needed to forgive and release, including herself for feeling like it was her fault even though she was just a young girl. I remember her asking, "Can I forgive God?" I remember questioning if that was theologically sound, but she felt she needed to express to God that she felt as though He had abandoned her at her moment of greatest need. If this is where you're at as well, then go for it. God can handle all our questions. If that is your tool to freedom, I am sure He will meet you in that place. My prayer partner asked her a powerful question next: "Where was Jesus during all this?" You see, the girl had had a vibrant relationship with God since she was very young. She knew His presence and was accustomed to following Him. She looked at us and began to weep. She said she pictured Him standing above her bed weeping with her but also protecting her with a giant shield between her and her stepfather, and that things could have been so much worse than what happened. This image brought great healing and relief to this girl's heart. I am not making light of this evil that she encountered. No one should have to walk through that. But what is beautiful is she decided she was not going to stay stuck or allow this abuse to be the thing she would pass down to her own children. She realized she was never alone, she realized God had prevented much worse from happening, and most of all, she realized how deeply loved she is.

There was an inner healing of freedom that took place in her heart, and she has never been the same since. Her relationships began to flourish, her trust in God was renewed, and her vision for life was stronger than ever. You do not need a counselor to walk through this type of deliverance, but this is a powerful tool for any area of your life you may feel stuck in. Allow the Holy Spirit to lead you and guide your thoughts and prayers out of any place of fear or torment, and into greater measures of His love.

One Step at a Time

"One step at a time" was the phrase that I would hear repeatedly in my spirit. I was definitely in the in-between season of believing God for my physical healing but not yet fully walking in it. I had dealt with the fear of it all and had moved forward into treating this thing. My faith was strong, and I was ready to be done with this chapter. God had led me to a clinic in Long Island, New York. It was very advanced in treating Lyme. It was one of my first days of treatments and I was in the in-between of disease to healing. I have never been a big fan of needles, and I remember they had to find the right vein to be able to stick the IV in. I whispered a little prayer, *"God, please help. Show me You are with me. Would You love on me extra today?"* By this point, I had learned that the opposite of walking in fear was living more in the love of God. I sensed that still, small voice whisper, *"Jaime, My daughter ... one step at a time."* I knew the next step was getting this first IV in and me being able to get through it. It took several stabs, but they finally succeeded. One down and about thirty more to go, all within the next three months.

About twenty minutes in, a young man, who happened to be handsome (which clearly distracted me!), caught my attention and sat down in the IV chair next to mine. I recognized his voice, and his face was also familiar. After about five minutes of trying to figure out who this was, it clicked. This was the guy in the video testimony I saw! He overcame Lyme disease at this clinic. He must have been ten years older now. One of the reasons I chose this clinic was because of this specific guy's story of overcoming the disease thanks to the doctor who was now treating me. I remembered thinking, *Wow, what are the chances he would be here? What is he doing here? Is he sick again?* Before I let my mind go to too many places, I began to chat with him. I shared how it was my first day there and his story was so impactful in my life. He began to encourage me and offer hope in the healing treatment journey I had just begun. He was there getting a "tune-up." As I listened, I was undone by how much God is in the smallest of details. He lived a few hours away and just happened to be there that same day, sitting next to me. Talk about a divine appointment and being loved on by God. Any bit of fear or anxiety that may have been lingering began to melt away as I thought of how sovereign our God is to line something like this up. It was the boost of faith my spirit needed, and the confirmation that I was in the right place at the right time. I wish I could tell you from that day forward I had zero fear, but what I can tell you is that my faith and courage muscles began to grow stronger and stronger every day. Instead of walking in that clinic afraid, I would walk in knowing the goodness and glory of God were with me. I would listen to worship music in my earbuds and sense the presence of God filling those small treatment rooms, sometimes stronger than any church service I had ever been in. God wants to lavish us with His love, but are we aware of and open to it? He can meet us in any place at any time, so let's be more aware of Him in everything and everywhere.

What is the next step you might be sensing God asking you to take in order to release fear from your life? Have you felt the weight of anxiety trying to creep in on you? When navigating a season that is not where you want it to be yet, there are many opportunities to give in to the worry of what could or will be. We also must guard ourselves from any complacency when nothing seems to be changing. This is fertile ground and a time to be aware of the enemy's tactics. I have learned to read the signs of the seasons. What I mean by this is I can now begin to tell when I am heading down a slippery slope of anxiety, self-pity, or depression. There are circumstances in all our lives that can trigger this. I have found that if I just forge ahead, even when my heart is aching, and not deal with those emotions, or become overly busy, I cannot really feel what is going on. Then I end up living a life that looks full on the outside but is hurting and empty on the inside. This will look different for everyone, but I can tell when I am starting to ignore the things I do not understand instead of sitting with God and allowing Him to walk me through it. When was the last time you really sat with God and allowed Him to speak to your heart and lead you through any emotions that are causing distress? Don't just push them aside and ignore them or get sucked into distractions like social media or Netflix, or anything else that may take you away from how the Lord wants to meet with you in that tender place.

We all know how important good communication is in relationships, but it is even more important with the Lord. Are you taking the time to listen to what He has to say or just moving ahead with what you want Him to say? Doing a heart checkup is very wise and will help you guard against fear taking over your life. Evaluate how you really are. Not how things look on the outside but how you are doing on the inside. Some may call this being self-aware, but I like the term *spirit-aware*. Knowing where I am with the Holy Spirit and asking if I am in step or out of step emotionally, spiritually, and physically.

As a believer, I think it is important we are *others* focused as much as we are focused on ourselves, but there are times in all our lives where we must check in and see if we are on track, in step, and aware of how we come across to people. Spirit-led self-awareness will help with this. One of the roles of the Holy Spirit is to guide and lead us into all truth. Ask the Holy Spirit to make you more aware of Him and how He is molding and shaping you.

One of the roles of the Holy Spirit is to guide and lead us into all truth.

You might notice some patterns in your life as you dig a bit deeper in this area. I have noticed that before any season where fear hit me, I typically ended up being burned out—whether that was from an out-of-balance work or ministry life, not taking great care of myself emotionally or physically while on the road, not dealing with inner heart issues relationally speaking, or a physical ailment or sickness. There are many times in our lives, especially if you are a female, where hormonal changes can also play a role in chemical shifts that cause anxiety. Being aware of this and evaluating where you are will better help you know how and what to overcome and work on. If God is the author of love, then you can imagine the enemy loves to counteract that with fear. This can manifest in many ways in our lives that I'd love to look at a little deeper.

If you have ever felt paralyzed in your decision-making process, then you could be operating out of a spirit of fear. God has given each of us a sound mind, so if you are always indecisive, then you might doubt yourself or your ability to make good decisions. This comes from a root of fear that can absolutely be broken off of your life.

If you have ever felt as though you needed to take a step forward, but you felt stuck or paralyzed, then you might be operating in a spirit of fear. The enemy loves to keep us stagnant, but the kingdom of God is full of forward movement in Christ and becoming all He has purposed us to be.

Perhaps you know that you need to address an issue with someone, but you would rather just avoid the whole thing and shrink back. This is called avoidance, and you might be operating out of a spirit of fear if this keeps haunting you. Walk strong in the discernment and wisdom God has given you and do not let someone intimidate you into shrinking back.

Many people know that God has called them to a specific assignment, but they have believed the lie that they are not ________ enough. I would wonder if fear is at work in the soil of your heart, holding you back from what you know you are truly called to do.

This list could go on and on, but I wanted to expose some of the ways we might be walking in fear and not even recognize it.

Faith > Fear

The opposite of fear is faith, so one of the best ways to move out of fear is by learning a deep dependence on and trust in God. Fear doesn't necessarily indicate a lack of faith. There are times where it signifies a lack of feeling safe. Choosing faith over fear is an adventure where we cultivate faith as a discipline. Having faith in God over fear is where we trust in God's plan and provision even during times of uncertainty, trials, and danger. We must first acknowledge and face our fears but not allow them to control or consume us. Instead, we can choose to lean on God's promises and character, believing that He is faithful and kind, and that He is with us through all of life's ups and downs.

Having faith in God over fear is where we trust in God's plan and provision even during times of uncertainty, trials, and danger.

When we are dealing with any kind of emotional fear, this shows us an area our minds need to be renewed with the Word of God. If we deal with a spirit of fear, it is an indicator that we have an enemy that wants to steal, kill, and destroy us. So how can we decide to choose faith over fear when we are dealing with one of the above?

Fear is a direct result of sin. After the fall, we lost our safe dwelling place, which was to be one with God. We became slaves to sin, and our father became the devil, who is full of lies. Feeling safe is one of the greatest needs for the human heart to thrive and live out a full life. True safety comes from knowing where we stand with God. We are at ease and rest in the palm of His hands no matter what this life might throw at us. There is a quiet confidence and trust in who He is that we can rely on.

Questions we need to ask ourselves: What are we trying to bear that Jesus bore? Is there an area that we are trying to control instead of releasing all control and truly surrendering it all to Jesus?

I wanted to end this chapter with tips and practices that you can put into place if you are someone who is prone to more fear and anxiety in your life. These are some practical tools to help you along the way.

1. Seek godly counsel. Don't be afraid to reach out to someone who is a little further down the road in their faith walk. Maybe a trusted friend, mentor, or pastor. Walking by faith does not mean we have to walk it out alone. Surround yourself with people who will hold you accountable and are more concerned with your growth in the Lord than anything else.

2. Walk in total surrender. Surrendering all control unto God means that we no longer trust in our ways or our plans. We lay down what we think or want to happen and trust in His sovereign will over our lives. This is not always easy. We want to hold on to things and believe God will make our plans come to pass. But true surrender will never be wasted in the eyes of God.

3. Spend time in prayer. One of the best ways to truly get to know the heart of God is by spending time with Him. Take time each day to reflect on God's character and promises, asking for His guidance and wisdom in your life. Journaling, reading Scripture, and listening to worship music can also be helpful in cultivating a deeper connection with God.

4. Embrace God's timing. Trust that this is a journey, not a sprint, of learning how to overcome fear and truly walk by faith. There is no rushing in the kingdom of God. He has a perfect time and place for everything. You might need to shift to a long-term perspective and stay committed to your growth in this area.

5. Take a step of faith. Is there something God is asking you to do? Take that first step of faith in obedience to Him and watch what He will do with it. Actions over words, as this might involve taking risks or facing challenges. God will provide exactly what you need.

A Prayer to Overcome Fear

Dear God, I can see areas of my life where I have cracks in my foundation and have allowed fear to creep in where You are wanting Your love to overflow. I open my heart, mind, soul, and spirit up to You now and ask that You would fill me with more of the perfect love of Jesus. Would You highlight and reveal to me any areas I have allowed in or opened the door to a spirit of fear? I want to close those doors now and walk in faith and dependance on You. Would You show me how much You love me today in details that only You and I would know about? Would You cause my faith to increase as I take bold steps forward in faith? I ask You to heal and deliver me from any anxiety that has taken hold of me from not dealing with the root of fear. As I open myself up completely to You, would You fill me with the unconditional love of God? Show me any areas of my life where I need to be Spirit-led and aware? Help me walk in a posture of faith over fear.

In Jesus' name.

Journal

Chapter 10

WILL YOU WAIT WELL?

Patience is something I have been forced to learn. We all have dreams and hopes that we are waiting to see fulfilled. As you probably picked up on by now, I've had to learn to be patient in three of the biggest areas in life: family, career, and health. But I feel I have learned the secret to waiting well. If you surrender your timing, then you no longer feel like you are waiting. I believe wholeheartedly that when I put my time frame on what I am praying for, and months or years pass without anything happening, then I end up feeling like I am waiting forever. Instead, I have learned to live in faith that it WILL happen. But in the meantime, I can either get busy living in the present while also taking steps forward toward that desired thing, or I can continue to do nothing while waiting.

It took me a while to figure this out, but in the Scriptures, the word *wait* means "to hope, to anticipate, and to trust." To hope and trust in the Lord requires faith, patience, humility, meekness, long-suffering, keeping the commandments, and enduring to the end. Whew, those are some intense words that are not always easy to walk out! Hope is so closely tied to waiting because we are hoping for something to happen. Without hope we won't be able to wait well. So we must make sure we are stewarding our hearts in a meek and trustful manner unto the Lord. I don't know what it is about getting older, but I find little things that never used to bother me really get on my nerves now. One of my least favorite places to wait is at the DMV ... Jesus, take the wheel (literally). I do not know what your DMV is like, but we have an incredibly outdated system here, the longest lines no matter what time you go, and customer service that needs some Chick-fil-A training. If you know me, that is the only thing I like about Chick-fil-A: the customer service! Ha ha! I told you I'm crunchy!

When you know your end point and destination, then it is much easier to wait. But where confusion runs wild you begin to feel aimless, just as I did in the corner of the DMV as every last seat was taken. We need a mental plan as we wait, or we will become increasingly frustrated. One day I decided I was going to write down everything I was waiting on and what I would do once those prayers and dreams came to pass. What I realized was that I could start doing more than half of them now. I didn't have to wait for some future "someday" to happen. It was going to take some planning and hard work to get there, but if God was giving me the green light, then why just sit around and think that my Uber Eats delivery guy was my future husband who would take me to Italy instead of just going solo? I began to write out all the places I wanted to travel to even if that meant going alone or with friends. Then I took those trips.

There are a few spots on my list that I feel led to wait to travel to until I am married, but that is personal between the Lord and me, and it makes the wait even better. What this practice did was give me so much hope and something to look forward to.

The trap of the enemy is to make us feel like we are going in circles as we wait. This can begin to paralyze us to not move at all. From a biblical standpoint, God tells us over and over again that our steps have been ordered by Him. Psalm 37:23 says, "The steps of the righteous are ordered by God." This tells me that we should get moving and take the first step. I think most unfulfilled potential is due to never trying. This comes down to one question: Are we truly being obedient to the Lord?

Are there areas where you are not waiting well? Do you feel like the art of patience is something you really need to hone? Let's take a look at what the Bible has to say about walking in patience. Psalm 37:7 says, "Rest in the LORD, and wait patiently for Him; do not fret" (NKJV). Waiting could cause us to be anxious and impatient because it seems like God isn't doing anything. However, we must remember that He loves us and gives good guidance, provision, help, and strength during the wait. There is nothing out of

His reach, so if He is asking us to wait on something then there is a greater purpose and plan.

So why does God put us in situations where we have to wait? First, and most foundationally, He uses waiting to increase our trust in Him and to loosen our perceived control. Waiting reminds us we're at the literal mercy of God's timing, and we have no power to change that. As humans we crave control, yet waiting pulls that from our grasp. I know you might be thinking, *But I do not deal with control issues.* Can I challenge you that if you are having a hard time waiting on something, then you might be trying to control the timing and outcome of it. Once again, this brings us to that openhanded, openhearted posture of surrender. It really is our greatest gift to let go and allow the Spirit of God to loosen our grip so that we can wait with joy for what the Lord wants to do in our lives.

There are times we can confuse patience with long-suffering and, many times, these two can go hand in hand. I can definitely say that when I was walking through my health journey, it felt very long, and I was genuinely suffering in different ways. Waiting can feel the same ... it can be tiresome, and you may feel as though you do not understand why God is making you wait. As Christians, we must be long-suffering. Paul wrote in Ephesians 4:2, "With all lowliness and meekness, with longsuffering, forbearing one another in love" (KJV). We must follow the advice of Paul in Colossians 1:11 and 3:12, "Strengthened with all might, according to his glorious power, unto all patience and longsuffering with joyfulness.... Put on therefore, as the elect of God, holy and beloved, bowels of mercies, kindness, humbleness of mind, meekness, longsuffering" (KJV). I am not saying any of this will be easy, but I do think it is a place of spiritual maturity when we can begin to wait well.

Preparation in the Waiting

Instead of believing that you are at a standstill as you wait for a promise to come to fruition, you can begin to ask how to prepare for the season or thing you are desiring to come to pass. For many of us women, we constantly dream of our wedding day and what that will look like. I will never forget being on a flight and literally laughing out loud as I was dreaming into that day and talking to the Lord about how I hoped it would be. I was in my early forties and had put on a few extra stubborn pounds, but was happy regardless. As I was picturing my special wedding day, I kept seeing a dress in mind and what I would look like in it ... as well as my honeymoon attire! I realized the vision I was seeing that dress and attire in was from my early twentysomething figure. I sensed the Holy Spirit kindly say, *"You may need to start exercising again if you want to look like that,"* and literally laughed out loud. I knew it to be true, but the little nudge from the Holy Spirit to start getting in shape again did not hurt. This was an area that I could begin to get prepared in. I have a vision and goal in mind as I am typing now. I am laughing thinking about the different style dresses, various wedding venues, and even types of guys I thought I was going to marry along the way.

Oh, how God's plans are best and how we grow and mature in Him. Are there areas that you might begin to prepare yourself for? I meet a lot of young people who have a desire to speak or teach in ministry, which is awesome. Are you preparing yourself now for the weight of what you will need to carry in that season? Are you allowing your character to be sharpened in the current season and growing close with the Lord in private, so you have something to say when He gives you that public stage? Will you be able to carry the weight of a platform, or will it take you out? Or perhaps you cannot wait to be a mom. There are so many things in the natural that you can begin to do to prepare for that. I have a friend who waited and waited to be a mother. She married young, but it took a while for them to conceive. She felt in her spirit that God wanted her to prepare her home for children. She began to clean out closets and literally put together a nursery for a baby. She bought the crib and the clothing, and felt like she should be fully prepared for when that day came. I wish I could say it all happened overnight, but when it did happen, she was prepared. Even more than that, she knew she had obeyed the Lord in the way He was leading her.

As a singer-songwriter, I have the privilege of writing many songs. Sometimes I wonder if these songs will ever be published or if anyone will ever even hear them. In order to make an album, you usually comb through and pick the best ten or so songs from your catalog. There have been many seasons where I wondered why I was still writing, with thoughts such as *Am I really going to release another album? I am indie now. Most labels are signing twenty-year-olds. God, is this a waste of time?* This is another example of why it is so important to be prepared in the waiting. I kept my head down and kept giving it my all during cowriting, wondering if anyone would ever record these songs or if I would ever make an album again. Then something seemed to happen out of nowhere but was a complete God setup. A new project with a new label and new songs. I am so grateful I was prepared with a catalog of songs we could listen through as well as the creative ability to write new ones.

We can also be prepared for when harder times hit. Have you ever sensed the Lord asking you to do something that made no sense at the time, but you can look back and see that it was not only preparation but it was also protection? I am not the best planner (I blame my creative brain for that!), but there have been many times where I knew God was asking me to plan out something in preparation for what was coming.

Who knows what He is setting up for you in the future that you might not be able to see right now. How do we prepare for something we are not even sure will come to pass? First and foremost, it is by having a heart posture of faith. God feeds on faith while the devil feeds on fear. We do not need to beg God for anything, but we do need to position our hearts, souls, and minds in a manner that shows we trust and believe that however and whenever He chooses to bring something to pass, it will be in our best interest. The second way you prepare is by resting in Him. By *resting in Him*, I mean your heart is not striving but is at peace that God is in control. This is difficult for many of us to do because we think we can simply ignore that heart posture, strive to get it done, figure it out on our own, and work our way to that desired goal, all the while our efforts will end up being a vain attempt to bring something to pass before its God-ordained time. I do not want the right thing at the wrong time because it would be the wrong thing. Have you ever read this quote?

It has always resonated with me and holds biblical truth. "The right thing at the wrong time is the wrong thing" is a reminder that doing the right thing at the wrong time, or in the wrong way, is still wrong. It can also be a lesson that mistakes made for the right reasons can take years to unravel.

God feeds on faith while the devil feeds on fear.

Let's do a deep dive on this topic taken from an online study I completed by Bryce Staggs, one of the staff members at Rocky Creek Church.

> In Exodus 2, we begin to see the life of Moses unfold. Moses was born to Levite parents and was set apart to be a mediator between Israel and God (Exodus 2:1–10). While he lived 40 years in the Pharaoh's palace, he never forgot where he came from. He never forgot the Hebrew people (Exodus 2:11). Moses was ready to intervene for God's people. In Exodus 2:12–15, Moses tried to deliver a Hebrew from the rule of the Egyptians. Moses ended up killing the Egyptian and having to run to Midian.

Moses' heart was in the right place. He was called to deliver the Hebrews, and that's exactly what he was trying to do. So what was the problem? Moses tried to act under his own power. If Moses had delivered the Israelites at this moment, God would not have gotten the glory, and Moses would have been the hero.

This serves as a truthful reminder: The right thing at the wrong time, done in the wrong way is the wrong thing.

Of course, God wants us to do the right thing. But not only should we strive to do the right thing, but we must also strive to do it at the right time. Trusting in God's timing, not our own. Additionally, we must strive to do the right thing in the right way. Moses was attempting to deliver the Israelites (doing the right thing), but his timing and method were under his own hands, not God's.

When God calls us to do something, we must continue to listen to Him and be guided by Him so that we ensure we continue to follow the path laid before us. Too often, we see where we need to end up and try to get there on our own.

Don't stop listening to God; when things try to take you off the path, press on. God is at work.[1]

The Art of Patience

In the New Testament, the virtue of patience is called a "fruit of the Spirit," or the evidence of the presence of the Holy Spirit in our lives (see Gal. 5:22). As such, we are to pursue growth, by the power of the Spirit, to become more patient with ourselves, with God, and with others. Every time I want to jump ahead in any area of life, I hear that gentle nudge of the Holy Spirit asking me, "Will you embrace the art of patience?"

It might be my least favorite "fruit" talked about in Scripture, as it is one of the hardest for most people to really lean into. However, I do believe there is a way we can navigate patience and begin to enjoy it. Think back to a time in your life when you had to really wait on something. When that situation finally came to fruition, you were probably rejoicing not only in the fact that it happened but in the supernatural ways it happened. I can remember the first time I went to the Gospel Music Association's annual Dove Awards. It is like the Grammy Awards for gospel and Christian music. I was twenty-five and had not been walking with the Lord for very long. I was given one ticket by a producer I was working with at the time and ended up going alone. I was told you could wear anything, but had I known most women would be in beautiful dresses, I would have dressed fancier. I chose the cute artist look with trendy jeans, heels, and a painted army-green jacket. What I didn't know when I showed up was that my ticket was in the second row with all my favorite artists, and I would be sitting next to Smokie Norful and his wife. One of his songs had impacted my life deeply, years prior. Was this real … was I dreaming?

The show was amazing, and the entire night I kept thanking God for the fact that I was even in the room. I had not yet released an album with a label but was on the road working on my first big label-supported album. At some point in the night, I had this sense that one day I would be nominated. It was the strangest feeling because, at the time, I honestly didn't care about "industry" things. Unfortunately, I got tied up in that world later in my career. But at the time, I brushed it off and thought there was no way it would happen and listed all the reasons I thought this. Years into my career, I never had any reason to go back to the awards. I was never nominated again while on that label, I was touring when the live show happened each year, and then I branched out as an indie artist. I had so many peers and friends who would get nominated, and I can remember celebrating them. A few of the years when I was in town, I even babysat for their children while they were at the show.

Throughout those years, God was working patience in me. Patience in His ways and timing that I was not even fully aware of. As time passed, there were certain seasons where desire for that kind of recognition among my peers would grow, but then as I took it to the Lord, I always sensed that it was more of an earthly accolade. Even though it would be nice to be at that level with my peers, my heart was content knowing I was doing what I was called to and doing my best to stay in the will of God, walking obediently with Him. It was not something I thought of often, until about five years into my career when I got invited to sing background vocals at the Dove Awards for Michael W. Smith. It was a fun experience, but I had completely forgotten about that little nudge those many years prior.

Fast-forward to twenty years later. I had released my first full-length album as an indie artist in over ten years. I was still healing from Lyme and had just begun touring again. That little desire and dream had been tucked so far down I never really thought it could happen. I got a random call from my music publisher in the summer of 2020 telling me that my new album was nominated alongside four others for Inspirational Album of the Year. He told me to find my dress because I would be walking the red carpet at the Dove Awards in October. I remember asking him if he was joking. Two of my favorite artists were nominated, as well as people who I had looked up to for so long. This could not really be happening.

Twenty years after I had sat in the second row with the Holy Spirit nudging my heart, this was happening in reality. I even sat close to that same seat, but this time as a nominated artist soaking it all in. I wish I could tell you I took home the award that night, but I didn't. What I did take home was a renewed sense that when God speaks, He moves. But, more times than not, it will be in a completely different way or timing than we could even imagine.

In the natural, this made very little sense. Most major-label artists are nominated through block voting within the industry, so the fact that enough people voted for my album *All Things* was amazing in and of itself. I had no real "team" at the time, but God did it. That is how you know when God speaks and wants something to happen, He will make it happen. If He could open blind eyes by spitting on mud, and if He could part the Red Sea, then there is nothing too hard for Him. The hard part comes when we do not want to wait on His process or ways to be worked out. The best part is that it never became something that was too "precious" to me. I think we need to be very careful as Christ followers to not place too much identity in what we do but, instead, to live openhanded in everything. How large our churches are, how many followers we have on social media, or how many people look up to us. Will any of that matter in eternity? So take a breath. Relax. It might not take twenty years for that thing you are believing for to come to pass, or it might. But I can tell you with all my heart ... it was RIGHT ON TIME for me.

When God speaks and wants something to happen, He will make it happen.

The biggest key I can offer you on how to wait well is to live fully in the present moment. Look at your life and see what is working and where you are thriving and jump into those places. For whatever reason, this is where God is moving in your life. I know the temptation to want what you are waiting on to happen as soon as possible, but why not enjoy the things that are blooming in this season? If you are single and waiting to meet your person, what if you enjoy the community of friends and family God has put around you? We all know that once dating, engagement, and marriage come, you won't have as much time to spend with those folks, so enjoy the gift of time you have with them now. I know many parents who have shared that when children were not being conceived in the time they had planned, they decided to fully embrace their season together and do the things they knew would be more challenging to do with a full household. They took a monthlong road trip working remotely. They booked trips around the world with no strollers needed. They invested financially in what they knew would have to take a back seat once their back seat was full of car seats. Was it easy all the time? No. We all will have longings as we wait that we have to surrender to the Lord. I am not saying that the desires will disappear, but until that appointed time comes, your focus will be not only on what you do not have but on all you DO HAVE. This is how we exchange our sorrow for joy; this is how we lay our disappointment at the feet of Jesus.

Habakkuk 2:3 says, "There is still a vision for the appointed time; it testifies to the end; it does not deceive. If it delays, wait for it; for it is surely coming; it will not be late" (CEB). If God has set something in motion in your heart but it has not yet come to fruition, will you begin to see it as a holy invitation to wait? The delay, and even the distractions, might very well be protection from the wrong things. Rest in His love, lean into what He is doing in your life in the present, and hold on to hope with everything you've got. "Though it tarries" ... wait! (Hab. 2:3 NKJV).

Now, I am in no way saying that waiting seasons are a cakewalk. In fact, I often joke with people that I have been at the head of the patience class for decades now! But every time my plans don't pan out, I see how much better it was when I waited on God's way and timing. When I'm on tour, I have a T-shirt on my merch tables that says, "Worship in the Waiting." I can say with all my heart worshipping God has become a weapon as I wait on the Lord to do the things only He can do. Maybe you need to begin to worship Him as you wait. Although I write about what to do in the waiting, I still want to acknowledge how hard, disappointing, and heartbreaking it can be at times.

We are human beings with very real God-given emotions. He wants us to acknowledge those emotions but also navigate the waiting with Him instead of shutting Him out, which can be tempting to do with any kind of disappointment. Something that's helped me is recognizing what my triggers are. Once you pinpoint those, then you can guard yourself from pitfalls of self-pity. Trust God in the process of growing in these areas. We are all a masterpiece in progress.

Here are several questions to reflect on and ask yourself while waiting:

1. Are you willing to lay down your timetable and trade it for how and when God chooses to move in your life?

2. Is there anything God is asking you to do in preparation for something you are waiting on? Make a list and begin to conquer those things one at a time.

3. Is there anything you could be doing now that you have been waiting for the right time to do, even if it looks a little different than you had planned?

4. When was the last time you embraced the art of patience and allowed that attribute of the Spirit to really grow in your life from a posture of faith and joy instead of dread and struggle?

Journal

Conclusion

A FINAL NOTE FROM JAIME

Dear new friend,

I pray as you have turned to these last pages that your heart is overwhelmed by the goodness, kindness, and faithfulness of God. No matter what season you find yourself in, He is right there with you and loves you more than you could ever fathom. My prayer is that your heart has been fortified and charged up to truly begin to embrace the beauty of the in-between you find yourself in. I wish we could sit down over a golden milk latte, and you could share all the ways you have sensed the Lord calling your heart into a deeper place of surrender and trust as you have read through this book.

May the questions and activities at the end of each chapter be something you go back to from time to time to evaluate where you are. I would love to encourage you to do some "heart checks" along the way to see if your grip is getting a little too tight again or if you are living in that openhanded posture of surrender.

I do not think any of us will ever "arrive" to the place of living this out perfectly until we are in heaven, where there will be no more waiting, wanting, desiring, longing, or in-between seasons. Everything will finally be fulfilled on that day of homecoming. Things that never happened here on earth and the sting of those disappointments will be wiped away with just one encounter in His presence.

I began this journey encouraging you to take a look at the "hard" in your life as a holy invitation into who God is creating you to be. To begin to view things with a new perspective. I hope you have been challenged to watch your words and what is coming out of your mouth, as it is a direct reflection of the state of your heart. We dug into the power of our thoughts and the daily practice of renewing our minds with the Word of God so that we can truly know who God says we are and live in a way that reflects that truth. These two tools will bring amazing growth in your life, so I hope you will watch your words and thoughts more as you continue to follow down the paths God has for you. If you felt like your hope had been hijacked in any way, may this be your reminder that hope is not in anything circumstantially but in the very person of Jesus. He is our living hope and the only one who can flood your life with abundance.

Although our plan A might not have happened, please continue to watch God work in a new way where plan B ends up being even better than you could have dreamed. I know if you read this entire book, God is wanting you to grow in some areas. I pray as He is shaping, molding, and pruning, you will feel how much He loves and adores you to not leave you stuck or stagnant. There are no shortcuts in the kingdom of God; it is our daily trust, obedience, and abiding in Him that will cause us to flourish into the men and women of God He has destined us to be. The next time you want to run ahead of the timing of God or fall back into complacency, I pray you would be reminded that God's timetable is indeed right on time. Learning to wait well is not something that will happen overnight, but in the days and months that pass, you will begin to see your growth.

May you tie gratitude and thanksgiving around your neck like a garment of praise. It will be one of your strongest tools as you navigate the in-between. Make it a practice every day and see how your life begins to flourish in every way.

I count it an absolute honor that you would take these words to heart and choose joy in your journey of waiting on God and living in a posture of true surrender. I would love to stay in touch and hear anything God spoke to you through this book, so feel free to reach out and find me on my social media accounts and keep me in the loop.

Maybe as you read this book you thought of someone who could use the encouragement and message from these pages. Would you share a copy with them? Perhaps you know a group of young women who would love to go through this together as a small-group study. I would love to hear how that goes!

Until our paths might meet again, enjoy every single step of this amazing God adventure. The ups and downs and everything in between are all working in and through us to make us more like Jesus, which is the ultimate goal of any season.

You are loved, you are seen, you are chosen. Live in that posture as you choose to live a sacred surrendered life.

All my love and blessings,
Jaime Jamgochian

If you would like to keep in touch with me, please visit my socials and website:

www.instagram.com/jaimejamgochian
www.facebook.com/jaimejamgochian
www.jaimejam.com
www.twitter.com/jaimejamgochian
YouTube: Jaime Jamgochian

ACKNOWLEDGMENTS

I am so grateful for this opportunity to write my first book. There are many people I would like to thank, but first and foremost, I give all glory and honor to God, who has been my constant strength and inspiration throughout the journey of writing this book. Without His grace and presence, these words would not exist.

Many of you know the Lord put it on my heart to do my very own "Eat, pray, love and WRITE" journey last summer. It truly was one of the sweetest journeys with God traveling to many favorite spots, and I literally felt like I wrote this with Him right by my side. Whether that was looking out at the gorgeous mountains in Banff, Canada, or the majestic sunsets on the beach in sunny California. Thank You, Lord, for such a fun summer of writing this book.

I am deeply grateful to my family—my mom, dad, and sister for their unwavering support and encouragement. Your prayers and love carried me through that season of writing. You guys have been my biggest champions throughout the years in full-time music ministry.

To my pastor, Alex and Henry Seeley, and all the amazing pastors who have spoken into my life over the years. Thank you for your spiritual leadership, your wisdom, friendship, and support over the years that have shaped much of what I've written here.

My heartfelt thanks to my literary agent, Debbie Alsdorf, for believing in this message and that I am not just a songwriter but deep down an author who had something to share. To my editor, Julie Cantrell, who treated this manuscript with care and insight, helping me refine the message straight from my heart. To Susan McPherson and the entire team at David C Cook–Esther Press, it has been an absolute joy to link arms with you all and work alongside to get this message out there.

To my close friends and prayer partners—you know who you are. I do not know where I would be without you. Thank you for believing in this calling and reminding me to keep the faith when doubt tries to creep in. Thank you for all the prayers and your sweet friendships. I feel so rich in community and love having you all in my life.

Finally, to every reader of this book: thank you for allowing my words to become part of your journey. May they draw you closer to the heart of God as you learn to wait well.

With much love,
Jaime Jamgochian

NOTES

Introduction

1. Jaime Jamgochian, vocalist, "Release," written by Tommy Iceland, Jessica Soccorsi, and Jaime Jamgochian, on *Sacred Surrender*, Curb/Word Music Publishing, 2023.

Chapter 2: Words Carry Weight

1. Music Education Works is a good hub for researching music's effects on a variety of people. See https://musiceducationworks.wordpress.com/.

Chapter 3: When Hope Has Been Hijacked

1. John Piper, "What Is Hope?," *Messages* (blog), Desiring God, April 6, 1986, https://www.desiringgod.org/messages/what-is-hope.

2. Definition of "hope" taken from "There Is Hope Today," Amy Lowe, *Christian Living* (blog), Thomas Nelson Bibles, October 4, 2023, https://www.thomasnelsonbibles.com/blog/there-is-hope-today.

3. "A Living Hope," *Hope (Devotionals)* (blog), Ligonier Ministries, April 5, 2005, ligonier.org/learn/devotionals/living-hope.

Chapter 4: God's Timetable Is on Time

1. Wikipedia, s.v. "kairos," last modified March 9, 2025, https://en.wikipedia.org/w/index.php?title=Kairos&oldid=1279626068.

2. Dictionary.com, s.v. "accelerando," https://www.dictionary.com/browse/accelerando.

Chapter 6: The Thoughts We Think

1. "Rumination: A Cycle of Negative Thinking," *APA Blogs* (blog), American Psychiatric Association, March 5, 2020, www.psychiatry.org/news-room/apa-blogs/rumination-a-cycle-of-negative-thinking.

Chapter 8: When God Wants You to Grow

1. "Study 5: The Little Foxes That Spoil the Vines," by Francis Dixon, *Bible Study Series: Series 33* (blog), Words of Life Ministries, https://www.wordsoflife.co.uk/bible-studies/study-5-the-little-foxes-that-spoil-the-vines/.

2. Craig Groeschel, quote taken from x.com, May 24, 2018, x.com/craiggroeschel/status.

3. Bible Study Tools, s.v. "qavah," https://www.biblestudytools.com/lexicons/hebrew/nas/qavah.html.

Chapter 9: More Love, Less Fear

1. "Anxiety Disorders," World Health Organization, September 27, 2023, https://www.who.int/news-room/fact-sheets/detail/anxiety-disorders.

Chapter 10: Will You Wait Well?

1. "When the Right Thing Is at the Wrong Time," by Bryce Staggs, Rocky Creek, https://www.rockycreek.church/resources/when-the-right-thing-is-at-the-wrong-time.

BIBLE CREDITS

Unless otherwise noted, all Scripture quotations are taken from the Holy Bible, New International Version®, NIV®. Copyright © 1973, 2011 by Biblica, Inc.™ Used by permission of Zondervan. All rights reserved worldwide. www.zondervan.com. The "NIV" and "New International Version" are trademarks registered in the United States Patent and Trademark Office by Biblica, Inc.™

Scripture quotations marked CEB are taken from the Common English Bible. Copyright 2012 by Common English Bible. All rights reserved.

Scripture quotations marked ESV are taken from the ESV® Bible (The Holy Bible, English Standard Version®), copyright © 2001 by